PRAISE FOR *FLAIR*

"*Flair* does quite an unusual thing by introducing a new word to the management literature – one that is both useful and, thankfully, not too difficult to put into practice. Jim and Jennifer Poage have done a fine research job in presenting exemplars of using flair and how valuable flair proves to be in designing and promoting products and services as well as boosting sales and delighting customers. A very interesting book well worth the reader's attention."

— LAURENCE PRUSAK, Consultant on knowledge management, former Executive Director of IBM's Institute for Knowledge Management, author of numerous books, including *Working Knowledge, Knowledge in Organizations,* and *What's the Big Idea.*

"Success of our personal and professional communications with others depends upon capturing their attention and trust, and effective sharing of our ideas. The Poages describe a communication style – flair – that they show, through examples, has been successful in both inter-personal interactions and commercial campaigns. They identify key elements of effective flair and provide useful guideposts and practical examples to help the reader adopt this style. In future, I intend to employ flair in my personal and professional interactions."

— L. PATRICK (PAT) GAGE, former President of Wyeth Research and Genetics Institute; former CEO of PDL BioPharma; Board Chairman of several biotech companies; and consultant in biotech.

FLAIR

FLAIR

Design Your Daily Work, Products,
and Services to Energize Your
Customers, Colleagues, and Audiences

JIM POAGE
JENNIFER POAGE

MAVEN HOUSE

Published by Maven House Press, 4 Snead Ct., Palmyra, VA 22963;
610.883.7988; www.mavenhousepress.com.

Special discounts on bulk quantities of Maven House Press books are available
to corporations, professional associations, and other organizations. For details
contact the publisher.

While this publication is designed to provide accurate and authoritative
information in regard to the subject matter covered, it is sold with the
understanding that the publisher is not engaged in rendering legal, accounting,
or other professional service. If legal advice or other expert assistance is
required, the services of a competent professional person should be sought.
— From the Declaration of Principles jointly adopted by a Committee of the
American Bar Association and a Committee of Publishers and Associations

Library of Congress Control Number: 2015917616

Paperback ISBN: 978-1-938548-39-0
ePUB ISBN: 978-1-938548-40-6
ePDF ISBN: 978-1-938548-41-3
Kindle ISBN: 978-1-938548-59-8   **33614059679851**

Printed in the United States of America.

10 9 8 7 6 5 4 3 2 1

DEDICATION

To Joanne, Jeff, Jon, and Nhu-Y for their

constant love and support.

CONTENTS

ACKNOWLEDGEMENTS

WE EXPRESS MUCH APPRECIATION for our agent, Ken Lizotte and his colleague Elena Petricone, of Emerson Consulting Group, for supporting our book idea and finding us potential publishers. We also give a great thanks to our publisher Jim Pennypacker of Maven House Press for believing in our book on Flair and for working along side us to turn our vision into reality.

Many family members and friends deserve a big thanks for their time spent listening to our evolving concepts and providing suggestions for improving our depiction of Flair. Jeffrey L. Poage, in particular, contributed by suggesting improvements for depicting flair in several examples, editing content, and giving insights into readability.

Thanks to those who provided their time for interviews and answered our probing questions: Steve Lenox of Lyons/Zaremba, Dominique Fillion of Reebok, Boris Esterkes of adidas, Richard Banfield of Fresh Tilled Soil, Mark Bartels of StumbleUpon, Deborah Abel of Deborah Abel Dance Company, Chris Newth of the Museum of Fine Arts Boston, and Charlie Davidson of The Andover Shop in Cambridge, Massachusetts. Appreciation also to those who provided pictures or comments: Trish Witkowski of Foldfactory.com; Michael Sawyer and Katie Berry of Fort Hill Group; Jack Levy; Ben Frankenberg of Bosie Tea Parlor in New York City; Fraser Currie of L.A. Burdick Chocolate Shop & Café in Cambridge, Massachusetts; Al Jacobson; Benson P. Shapiro, Professor Emeritus of Harvard Business School; and Yu-Chi "Larry" Ho, Professor Emeritus of Harvard University, School of Engineering and Applied Sciences.

INTRODUCTION

WHY DO SOME SMARTPHONES INSPIRE CUSTOMERS to wait in line overnight to buy their latest versions, while other tech device launches flop? Why do some clothing stores attract a steady stream of trendy patrons, while other stores see lackluster sales? Why do some briefings at work energize audiences to act, while others deflate the room? Generally stated, why do some offerings excite, while others fail to inspire? We found ourselves intrigued by these questions, and our subsequent research and analysis to find answers culminated in this book. We want to help everyone design offerings that excite.

Through our observations of successful products, services, and individual work, we concluded that to be successful an offering must engage customers, colleagues, and audiences emotionally and excite them to pursue the offering. This excitement results from what we call *flair*: an engaging element built into or around the offering that captivates customers, colleagues, and audiences. Throughout this book we'll show you that, for products and services, effective flair brings increased sales at a premium price and fosters an enduring positive reputation. For your everyday work, effective flair inspires colleagues and audiences to follow up on your results and recommendations – you'll stand out and your work will be memorable, which will help you to move ahead in your career. By *effective* flair we mean that the flair energizes your customers, colleagues, and audience *to act* – to buy, adopt, or follow up on your offering.

Jim's journey to understanding and using flair in his work began a dozen years ago. He wondered if the practices of the companies who succeeded at flair could be applied to his consulting work. Could he make his results, reports, and presentations more engaging to clients? Could he go beyond doing *good* work and provide *energizing* work? At a workshop by Stephen Denning, Jim was exposed to storytelling as a way to explain to employees the benefits of organizational change. Storytelling, in this application, meant telling anecdotes about how the organization could function if it improved its practices. Jim thought, why not present his analyses as stories that showed how implementing his results would provide value to his clients? After receiving praise from clients for explaining how his results would work as well as for the clarity of his results, Jim extended his storytelling to enable his clients to experience – to see, to visualize – how their work would be conducted and enhanced if they used his results.

Jim's daughter Jenn learned about and used flair when she studied art and fashion design in college and graduate school and in her career in the fashion industry. While studying art history as an undergraduate at Drew University, Jenn learned that memorable art engages the viewer emotionally, provokes further thought, and adds to the evolution of art. Her understanding of these principles of art and design was enhanced during her further studies in fashion design at Parsons School of Design, where she learned to meld elements of flair with good business practices to succeed as a creative person in the retail clothing industry. In her several years of working as an apparel technical designer for Reebok and adidas, Jenn put these methods to practical use, and she observed how effective flair in products, marketing, and daily work improved sales, profits, and career advancement.

We became intrigued by seeing how similar companies could be so different in evoking an emotional response from their customers. We began our collaboration by discussing how the techniques used in creative fields, such as fashion design, exhibit design, and graphic design, could be adapted to almost all products and services to engage customers emotionally as well as rationally. These discussions resulted in the idea for this book: to provide an understanding of what effective flair is, and explain the practices used to create that flair. Together we interviewed experts and researched companies that excel at building flair, such as a well-known athletic wear company, a firm that designs exhibit space, a fine arts museum curatorial manager, and a firm that designs web and mobile user experience interfaces.

From our research on what makes effective flair, we concluded that it's based on a product, service, or work result having a *meaningful and joyful essence*. The essence is what your offering brings to customers, colleagues, and audiences that causes them to find the product, service, or work result desirable. With a *meaningful* essence, they will feel a rational need for your offering – feeling that it's useful to them. With a *joyful* essence, they'll want your offering on an emotional level – convinced that it will make them happy.

Defining the essence of an offering isn't the same as simply listing its features – instead it's understanding what these features enable customers to do and how the offering makes them feel. For example, users of Apple's iPod can listen to music anywhere. Thus, we don't define the iPod's essence as storing and playing music but as "the joy of music is always with you." With this essence understood, Apple concentrated on designing the iPod to provide the enjoyment of music anywhere at any time through an easy user experience. The iPod's essence – "the joy of music is always with you" – is meaningful since customers can have access to their music library on the go, and it's joyful since music delights listeners.

Flair is a subjective quality that, along with other attributes such as organizational culture, branding, and collaboration, is part of any successful organization. Due to its intangible and fluid nature, we can't just say "do this and you'll have effective flair." Instead, we gathered methods from our interviews with creative professionals, who incorporate flair for a living, and from researching companies that understand effective flair. We then assembled our findings into a four-step process that anyone can use to add flair to any offering. Each step is thoroughly examined in this book, which includes real-life business examples and ideas on how you can easily incorporate this process into your own work.

Our interviews and research also revealed six elements of flair to be used as building blocks in creating effective flair: story, entertainment, experience, sincerity, excellence, and energy. Each of these elements is discussed in detail with an explanation of how it contributes to building flair in your offerings.

We conclude this book by showing you that you'll have fun when you strive to add flair to your own work and to your company's products or services. You'll delve into creativity, learn new skills, and gain further insight into your projects. And, most importantly, you'll see your customers, colleagues, and audiences excited by your work.

Note to Readers

Throughout this book we refer to customers, colleagues, and audiences. Sometimes, for simplicity, we combine them under the umbrella term *customers*. We also refer to clients, consumers, and users, and these are also included under this umbrella. Potential customers, prospects, and internal customers also fall under this umbrella. We also use the term *offering* throughout the book. Offerings can include products, services, or daily work results, such as reports, memos, and presentations.

PART I

A Meaningful and Joyful Essence – The Basis of Flair

1

Flair Sells

The essential difference between emotion and reason is that emotion leads to action, while reason leads to conclusions.

— Donald Calne, neurologist,
author of *Within Reason*

Flair Sells Products

 Just look at Beats by Dr. Dre headphones, which came on the scene in 2004 and quickly captured the market as the hip, trendy, and necessary way to listen to music. Rock music has always been about a rhythmic, captivating bass, and the Beats sound enhances the drive and energy of rock, hip-hop, and pop. Previous high-end headphones were tuned to produce an even sound across the music audio range and didn't provide a dramatic sound for pop music. Beats headphones do. In the May 2014 issue of *Inc.* magazine Burt Helm quotes Jimmy Iovine, co-founder of Beats along with Dr. Dre, saying: "We wanted to recreate that excitement of being in the studio. That's why people listen."[1]

Besides a dynamic sound that drives and pulses, Beats has a unique, bold, and fashion-forward look. So iconic in design, Beats has become a ubiquitous fashion accessory for pop culture celebs, sports stars, and trendy music lovers. Compared to Beats headphones in glossy, bright hues with a stylish wide headband and padded ear pieces, other brands, with muted, neutral colors, are lackluster tech rather than a fashion item. The Beats logo, on the side of each earpiece, is distinctive with a simple *b* that jumps out in a contrasting color.

With the flair of a throbbing rhythm and an electric appearance, Beats gained 62 percent of the premium headphone market and 30 percent of the $1 billion-plus total U.S. headphone market by 2014.[2] The company was sold to Apple for $3 billion in 2014.[3,4]

 ### Flair Sells Services

Zappos, an online shoe and clothing store, features happiness: happy employees and happy customers. Call center sales representatives don't use scripts, and call times don't have limits. On December 8, 2012, the longest customer service call came in at 10 hours, 29 minutes, during which most of the conversation was about what it's like to live in the Las Vegas area, and, yes, the customer did buy a pair of Ugg boots.

Purchases are often sent overnight even though the website states from two to five business days, and Zappos offers free shipping and returns. This makes the online shopping experience comparable to trying on shoes in a store, since customers can order multiple sizes to check the fit and return a size that isn't right.[5]

Bringing happiness to both employees and customers, call center representatives make their own decisions on such topics as providing a refund on defective orders, and the reps send a dozen or so personal notes to customers each day.[6] New hires train for four weeks no matter what their job will be, and contact center employees train for an additional three weeks. All call center employees have their own workstations and can paint their walls to individualize their personal space.[7]

Repeat customers and word-of-mouth are the main reasons for Zappos' growth. Launched in 1999, Zappos' gross sales reached $1 billion in 2008, and the company was sold to Amazon.com for $1.2 billion a year later, in 2009.[8]

Flair Sells One's Daily Work Results

What makes Doris Kearns Goodwin's recent books on Lincoln, *Team of Rivals: The Political Genius of Abraham Lincoln,* and on Theodore Roosevelt, *The Bully Pulpit: Theodore Roosevelt, William Howard Taft, and the Golden Age of Journalism,* so compelling is the inclusion of additional historical characters with whom Lincoln and Roosevelt interacted, thus expanding the narrative beyond the typical one-person or family biography.[9] In *Team of Rivals,* for example, she covers Lincoln's cabinet members, who had been rivals of Lincoln, particularly in his presidential election campaign of 1860. For Roosevelt, she shapes her book around the friendship between Roosevelt and William Taft and their relationship with the press. The book tells how Roosevelt and Taft first became good friends, then had an intense split, and finally renewed their relationship. Goodwin's format expands the storyline of a single-subject biography to cover multiple individuals, their relationships, and their joint impact on events, so that her books stand out from other biographies. This format, added to her engaging writing style, provides flair that adds to the success of her books. *Team of Rivals* sold more than 1.3 million copies by 2012 and was the basis for Steven Spielberg's *Lincoln* film of the same year.[10]

Effective Flair

The above three examples show that effective flair brings uniqueness, excitement, and sales success. What constitutes effective flair, and how to create it, are the subjects of this book. By flair, we mean charm, panache, pizazz, taste, style, élan, dash, spirit, liveliness, and any other word that indicates something that excites your customers, colleagues, and audience. By *effective* flair, we mean the flair energizes your customers, colleagues, and audience *to act* – to buy, adopt, or follow up on your offering.

Effective flair isn't a hotel door attendant wearing a flamboyant outfit. It isn't restaurant wait staff asking, "Is everything all right?" It isn't a greeter saying, "Hello, welcome to our store," to everyone who enters. And it isn't putting 3-D, multi-color charts with graduated shading and glowing edges in a briefing. Effective flair doesn't just add something cute or colorful. Rather it enhances and sincerely reflects the offering – as shown by Beats, Zappos, and Goodwin. Effective flair is meaningful, in that it provides something useful, and is joyful, evoking a smile or a "wow" in acknowledgement that it's clever and stimulating.

The benefits of flair for products and services are obvious: increased sales at a premium price to energized customers. Flair in the content and form of studies, memos, reports, presentations – your daily work – may seem less identifiable, but with a few principles and a process almost anyone, in any situation, can add effective flair to their work. The benefits of such flair are that managers and colleagues will quickly understand your work and how to use it to create value. They'll be energized and want to use your results. Their responses will help you stand out and make your work memorable.

Flair is within reach of anyone and can be created for any product, service, or work endeavor.

Flair Can Be Everywhere

An article in *Vanity Fair* in March 2014, about the early days of the California Institute of the Arts in the 1960s and 1970s, quotes design student Brad Bird, describing what he learned from Professor Bill Moore.[11] "Design was all around you," Bird said, "and it was either good design or bad design. But it was everywhere, and in everything: manhole covers, laps, furniture, cars, ads in the paper – everything has elements of design in it." The examples in the quotation are about physical things, but the quote's spirit conveys that anything can have flair, which also includes services and your daily work.

Success with Flair, Disappointment without Flair

To begin the journey of understanding what effective flair is and how to create it, examples of a product, service, and daily work result *with* flair will be contrasted with similar offerings *without* flair. These cases show that positive results come from understanding what's important to the customer at an emotional level.

Products with and without Flair

Apple can be considered the poster child for style and flair. According to Walter Isaacson in his book *Steve Jobs,* when the first iPhone was nearing its launch, Apple CEO Steve Jobs went to see Jonathan Ive, head of Apple design, and declared that the phone's screen didn't look right.[12] He felt that the case overlapping the screen interfered with the display being the focus. So Jobs told Ive's design team that they needed to work nights and weekends to rectify the case design issue. The designers agreed with Jobs and did just that. The result was the now-familiar thin stainless steel bezel with the glass screen covering the whole front. Jobs's understanding of flair led to the iPhone's extraordinary success. Deciphering what Apple and others do to successfully differentiate themselves with flair will provide the insights you need to add flair to your own work.

An example of a product without flair, the Microsoft Surface RT tablet/laptop combo had disappointing sales when it was introduced in October 2012. The Surface RT could be used as a tablet, when the screen that contained the electronics was detached from the cover, or as a laptop, when the cover that hosted a keyboard was attached. This tablet/laptop combination didn't catch on in the marketplace. According to International Data Corporation (IDC), in the first quarter of 2013 Microsoft shipped 900,000 Surface devices, including the Surface RT and Surface Pro models, while Apple shipped 19.5 million tablets and Samsung shipped 8.8 million tablets, out of a total of 49.2 million tablets shipped.[13] The detached display was too large and heavy to function comfortably as a stand-alone tablet, and the keyboard was too awkward for efficient typing to operate as a stand-alone laptop. Two properties of keyboards that affect typing are key response, which is a positive mechanical feedback indicating that a key has been pressed, and travel, which is the distance a key needs to be pushed to enter the character. The Surface RT offered two cover/keyboard options, but both were so thin that they didn't provide the key response and travel of a typical laptop keyboard. Thus, the extensive typing one would do on a laptop was cumbersome. The tablet portion had a foldout stand on its back that propped up the screen on a desk or table. However, the foldout stand was difficult to use on a lap, so the Surface RT as a "laptop" didn't work very well on a lap. Microsoft aimed for a laptop/tablet combination, which seems like a good idea, but the product that resulted fell short. There was little flair in the physical design or functionality of the Surface RT to excite users.

Success eventually came with the Surface Pro 3, launched in June 2014, which was retooled as a high-performance device with its own market niche rather than a combo tablet and laptop that competed against both stand-alone tablets and laptops. Leo Sun observed on *The Motley Fool* website: "Microsoft's Surface had a rough start when it hit the market in October 2012, but customers eventually realized the device was more of an ultrabook than a tablet. Microsoft also heavily marketed the Surface as a productivity device for students and professionals, rather than going head-to-head against the iPad as a consumer tablet."[14] While Microsoft may still not offer the style and simplicity that's abundant in Apple devices, it has at least targeted a specific market niche with a tailored product.

Apple and Microsoft are very large companies with plenty of money and staff to build flair or, in the case of Microsoft, sometimes build flair, and they can afford to revise the design of their products near launch. But we don't believe for a minute that Apple's flair is beyond the reach of small and medium-sized companies with more modest resources. With appropriate understanding and know-how, any company can create flair without the immense resources that Apple applies.

Services with and without Flair

Now, let's consider services that do and services that don't have flair. Target is often described as selling "cheap chic" and was early to feature collaborations with famous and up-and-coming designers. These included over 800 Michael Graves designs ranging from a teakettle to a garlic press to a toilet brush, as well as one-time offerings by popular or emerging fashion designers, such as Missoni,

Phillip Lim, Peter Pilotto, and Marc Jacobs. These pop-up fashion collections often sold out quickly. Target's television ads conveyed that the retailer brought pizzazz to your life through style and color for your clothes and home, and that its products, and the feelings of delight that accompany them, were accessible to everyone.

After the 2008 recession Target shifted its marketing focus toward low prices and away from flair and joy. Shoppers abandoned Target. A new CEO, Brian Cornell, took over in August 2014. He brought back the "chic" to pair with "cheap," and Target's stock has revived by 30 percent to an all-time high, as of late winter 2015, during his leadership.[15]

Now consider JCPenney during Ron Johnson's reign as CEO, from November 2011 to April 2013. Johnson had previously served as the head of Apple's retail stores, which were phenomenally successful, reporting the highest per-square-foot sales of any retail chain and more than double the next highest. Good things were expected with Johnson bringing the Apple retail magic to JCPenney. But JCPenney sales fell nearly 29 percent over one year, and its share price declined to half its value during Johnson's tenure. Johnson was fired after only seventeen months as CEO.

What happened? Why didn't Apple's retail success come with Johnson to JCPenney? Johnson may not have understood retail department stores, but he also seemed to not have comprehended what made flair effective at Apple. Jobs preached "simplify" at Apple. But Jobs' simplification was meaningful to customers, which enhanced their emotional engagement to the brand. Apple stores had a simplified customer experience that was appropriate to its customers, who were buying products about which they had many questions. Upon entering an Apple Store, a greeter assigns you to a sales associate. The sales associate is knowledgeable about the Apple products, explains the offerings, completes your purchase, brings you the purchased item, and shows you how to use it. You deal with only one staff member at the Apple Store, unless you have technical questions or need repairs, which are handled at the Genius Bar at the back of the store. This customer experience is appropriate given the technical nature of Apple products and conveys that Apple products are special. Johnson also worked at Target when it began to feature designer products. He had a major role in Target's collaboration with designers, but he does not appear to have understood how to transfer this experience with flair to JCPenney, a different type of retailer.

At JCPenney, Johnson, likely thinking he was simplifying the customer experience, eliminated frequent sales and coupons to provide everyday low, fair pricing.[16] This simplified advertising and, supposedly, pricing for customers. But frequent sales were meaningful to and even desired by JCPenney patrons. Customers searched for items they wanted in each sale promotion – looking for sales wasn't complicated for JCPenney customers. Eliminating sales didn't attract new customers but lost existing customers. Johnson also simplified pricing by rounding prices ending in 99 cents up to whole dollars. But who cares about paying in whole dollars rather than a penny less with a price ending in 99 cents. Not JCPenney's customers. Even with a price in whole dollars, once tax is added, the bill is back to dollars and cents. Television ads featuring Ellen DeGeneres describing Johnson's initiatives were enjoyable and engaging, but the changes themselves weren't. Jobs understood that simplification needs to be meaningful to customers. Johnson didn't appreciate this nuance.

Daily Work with and without Flair

At work you've likely dealt with people who left their colleagues and audiences deflated. You've probably sat though presentations that were hard to follow or were just plain boring, even though the content may have been good and meaningful. You've also, no doubt, dealt with people who drain your energy. In these cases you were unlikely to follow through with what you'd heard since you weren't inspired. By putting flair in your work you'll avoid those situations – you'll be an energizer, not a de-energizer. Being an energizer isn't about being an extrovert – it's about making the content and format of your subject matter clear and stimulating. We define effective flair in daily work as energizing your audience to act on your output – to implement or investigate further. Effective flair will help you to move ahead in your career.

In the late 1990s NASA began a research program called Advanced Air Transportation Technologies, which was aimed at enhancing the efficiency and capacity of the nation's increasingly overloaded air traffic control system. NASA's goal was to develop computerized systems to aid air traffic controllers in managing taxiing, departures, and arrivals at airports, and in flying between airports. The challenge NASA faced as it developed these different projects was to figure out which were most effective and by how much, what deserved funding, and what would draw positive support from the FAA and the airlines.

NASA hired an aviation consulting firm to develop performance measures to determine the impacts of the research program on airport operations. The resulting proposed measures seemed at first glance to make sense. But as NASA managers began to evaluate their projects, they found the measures to be of little help in making decisions. And yet the NASA managers couldn't articulate what was wrong with the measures.

Having developed measures for aviation programs at the FAA, Jim, then working for the Volpe Center of the U.S. Department of

Transportation in Cambridge, Massachusetts, was asked to look at the problem. After probing the meaningfulness of the existing measures, Jim concluded that, despite covering a variety of impacts, the measures didn't show how each project would help relieve the capacity problems of the nation's air traffic control system. What NASA had was a basketful of measures without links to specific projects and goals. Missing was *how* the measures would support NASA's decision-making about what projects to fund. After he explained his findings to the NASA team, Jim was asked to develop new measures.

Working with NASA project managers, Jim concluded that the measures needed to tell a story – they needed to show the benefits that the projects contributed to the research program. He decided to construct a chart organizing the measures to show each project's contributions to the program's goals. The resulting hierarchical chart showed individual projects along the bottom with the projects connected to a middle layer containing groupings of surface operations projects, terminal operations projects, and en route operations projects. At the top of the chart were the overall program goals, such as increase capacity, reduce delays, and save fuel. Appropriate measures were developed for each level.

Exhibit 1.1 shows sample measures and projects for the NASA research program. Contrast the usefulness of this structured presentation, which tells the story about the contributions of individual projects, with a list of measures not tied to any project or goal.

Adding flair through storytelling went beyond just defining performance measures; it conveyed the measures in a form that provided information that was useful to NASA. Previously NASA had been asked, and had difficulty explaining, why research was

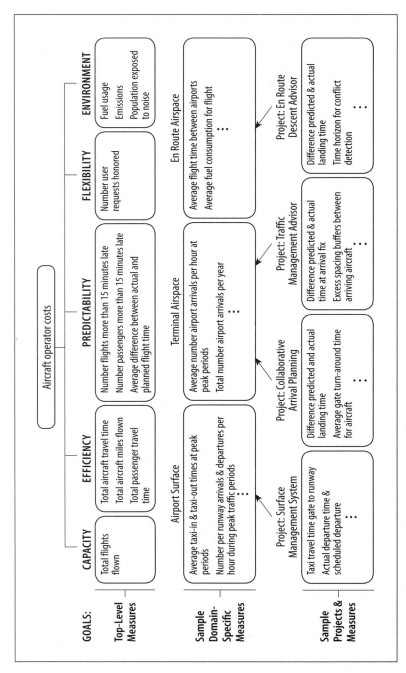

Exhibit 1.1. Chart tells a clear story about the contributions of NASA's aviation projects to overall program goals.

being conducted on projects that appeared to have little benefit. With this new narrative framework NASA was able to justify how a project in question was one step closer to a larger benefit and would enable following projects to provide significant value. The head of the NASA program said he was more comfortable presenting the research this way and that he appreciated Jim's work.

Some Questions About Flair

During the writing of this book, colleagues who helped review it raised several questions that may also occur to you. These questions are answered in the next few subsections.

Is Flair a Matter of Taste?

Yes, flair is certainly a matter of taste. What intrigues one person may be considered silly by another. For instance, we appreciate Apple's flair, but we don't always share the same tastes as Jobs. According to Isaacson's biography, Jobs personally selected the gray-blue Pietra Severna sandstone (which comes from a quarry near Florence, Italy) for the floors of the Apple Stores. Yet when Jim passes or enters the Apple Store at the Burlington Mall in Massachusetts, he doesn't immediately remember that the floors are stone and wonders why the Apple Stores have a dirty gray industrial carpet. He finds the gray-blue color and dull matte finish of the floors unattractive; to him they don't have the rich tonal qualities that some stone floors have. He also doesn't care for the very light-toned wood in the Apple Store tables, which he feels lacks the rich patina and grain often found in wood. The expansive white walls in Apple Stores are too minimalist for his taste. In contrast, Jenn finds the styling and presentation in the Apple Stores comfortable and refreshing. She feels comfortable inside and confident that she'll find sleek and technologically advanced products.

To achieve a successful offering, aim for flair that encompasses a wide range of tastes and is attractive to a significant portion of your target market. You won't please everyone, so don't let a small amount of criticism derail you from adding flair. In a 2006 *Financial Times* interview, Jay Leno described his first public performance as a standup comic, where he opened for the drummer Buddy Rich.[17] The emcee introduced Leno and asked the audience to welcome "a bright young comedian here called Jay Leno." Then someone in the audience shouted, "We hate him." Leno wondered how this person could hate him since he had never appeared anywhere. "Then I realized: you can't please everybody. You just have to do the best you can."

Is Flair Expensive, and Does It Require a Large Staff?

This book's thesis is that anyone can add flair to their products, services, or daily work if they understand what flair is. You don't have to be Frank Lloyd Wright, Michael Graves, or Steve Jobs to generate effective flair. However, some people, such as these individuals, do excel at design and flair beyond what most people can hope to achieve. If you can afford it, you probably want to hire skilled designers for important offerings. For many situations, however, hiring famous designers isn't cost-effective, so in the following chapters we present many methods that anyone can adopt.

Inexpensive product design with flair is possible. H&M, Zara, and Target feature stylish clothing that's reasonably priced. Inexpensive service with flair is also possible – it doesn't cost much for a restaurant or store to incorporate a warm and welcoming attitude that drives engaging service. The story format in the previously mentioned chart of measures for NASA doesn't require much more time to produce than a plain list. And of course you don't need to spend the effort to add flair when it doesn't matter.

Making tradeoffs between features and cost is part of most product development decisions, and the tradeoff between flair and cost is also part of these decisions. Designing for flair from the beginning of an effort is cheaper than adding flair toward the end. Later in this book we'll explain how to design for flair without great expense.

Does Adding Flair Require Changing the Culture of a Company?

One of Jim's friends agreed that flair was important and could be used at his company, but he believed that it would be hard to change the way his company operated in order to incorporate the emotional aspects of flair. But you don't have to change a company's culture to add flair. This book's content is aimed at helping people understand the nature of effective flair and how to create it. The practices we cover can be applied by one person or by a group to increase the likelihood their work will be memorable, appreciated, and adopted – in any workplace culture. Thus, an individual or team can begin to apply flair without cultural change. Just go ahead and try it – then watch the energetic response to your work.

How Much Flair Is Needed?

Someone with limited time and resources may wonder how much flair is needed to be effective. This is, of course, a judgment call. You don't want to keep the audience laughing continually throughout a business talk where a serious decision is to be made. You do want to engage the audience, but this doesn't mean that flair is needed throughout your entire talk. It can be added occasionally to vary the pace and tone of your presentation.

However, sprinkling flair throughout the entire user or audience experience is essential so that you don't set up an expectation that isn't later met. If you begin with flair and no more follows, your users or audience will be confused or even irritated that the high expectations set at the beginning didn't continue. For example, consider an experience shared with Jim by a colleague who heard an especially inspiring lecture. The speaker was dynamic, and the content was extremely interesting and clearly presented. It was one of the most energizing talks this colleague had ever attended. After the talk, a DVD of another talk by the speaker was for sale, so Jim's colleague purchased it for $100. Watching the video, he was quickly disappointed. The speaker wasn't dynamic or inspiring but instead droned on and on while standing in front of a blue background with no stage setting. He didn't finish watching it. Even after the memorable talk, the colleague was left with a low opinion of the speaker after receiving such a poor-quality follow-up DVD from him. Continue flair throughout your offering so you don't disappoint in the end.

Creating Effective Flair

The most important message of this book is that to create effective flair, a product, service, or work result needs to have a *meaningful and joyful essence,* a phrase that will be further explored as this book progresses. The essence is what an offering brings to customers, colleagues, and audiences that causes them to find it desirable emotionally as well as rationally. If this essence is meaningful to them, then they'll feel a need for your offering. If this essence is joyful, it will excite them or bring a smile to their faces, making the need emotional as well. In defining the essence, the focus isn't simply on the features but also on what these features enable customers, colleagues, and audiences to do and how the offering makes them feel. For example, Apple's iPod allows users to listen to music anywhere. Thus, our interpretation of the essence of the iPod isn't its ability to store and play music but that "the joy of music is always with you." With this essence understood, Apple concentrated on designing the iPod to provide the joy of music with a very simple user experience.

If the concept of a meaningful and joyful essence as the basis for flair isn't completely clear to you now, it will be by the end of this book. Chapter 2, in particular, is devoted to understanding the concept of essence. We don't think that it's particularly difficult to understand the essence of an offering, but rather that people often don't rigorously and methodically examine what their offering does for the customer emotionally as well as rationally.

Flair is one of those soft, subjective qualities that are part of successful organizations, along with such attributes as organizational culture, branding, human capital, and collaboration. Thus, we can't just say "do this, and you'll have effective flair." But people working in creative fields, such as fashion design and exhibit design, use structured processes to create flair; they don't wait for inspiration. These methods can be adapted by anyone to build a process that adds flair to any offering. Indeed, the approach summarized below and presented in Part III is derived from our interviews with designers in a variety of businesses, research on companies that create effective flair, and observations of occurrences of stimulating flair. We offer the following four-step process to help you create effective flair:

1. **Define a meaningful and joyful essence for your offering.**

   In Chapter 9 we'll describe how to keep asking, at progressively deeper levels, what your offering provides, until its essence is evident at an emotional as well as rational level.

2. **Add flair to achieve the meaningful and joyful essence.**

   In Chapter 10 we'll cover how to identify touch points where a customer interacts with an offering, identify what constitutes good experiences from the touch points, and develop flair to achieve the experiences.

3. **Validate that the flair is effective.**

   Since flair is imprecise, you may not hit truly effective flair in the first design iteration. Thus, validating the effectiveness of the flair and making revisions is good practice. In Chapter 11 we'll discuss validating for effectiveness, practicality of being produced, and possible negative reactions.

4. **Iterate among the first three steps.**

   In Chapter 12 we'll explain how you should iterate among these steps, rather than conduct them serially, for maximum flair.

Elements of Effective Flair

Our interviews and research revealed six elements of flair to be used as building blocks in creating effective flair. These six elements of effective flair are listed below. Since flair can't be precisely defined, others may have different lists, but the substance of the elements is likely to be similar. Your use of flair needn't incorporate all of these elements but should contain several.

Story   Tell a story about your offering.

Entertainment   Have your offering entertain your customers.

Experience   Create pleasant, even happy, customer experiences.

Sincerity   Construct flair to accurately reflect your offering.

Excellence   Be sure your offering is high quality so it doesn't disappoint.

Energy   Strive to energize your customers.

You can easily remember these points as SEESEE (the first letters of each element). Imagine exclaiming "See, see – this is flair!" when you deliver the joy of your product, service, or work result to enthusiastic customers, colleagues, or audiences. In Part II we show you how each of these six elements can be employed.

Essentials: Flair Sells

- Effective flair energizes, inspires action, and leads to sales success.

- Flair can be added to almost anything.

- Flair need not be expensive – just be selective on what flair to add.

- Anyone can design flair – with an understanding of effective flair and a process for creating it.

2

Understanding *Meaningful and Joyful Essence*

It don't mean a thing, if it ain't got that swing.

— Duke Ellington, composer-bandleader;
lyrics by Irving Mills

SEVERAL YEARS AGO Jim was viewing the *Impressionist Still Life* exhibit at The Phillips Collection in Washington, DC, when he came across a painting called *Study of Flowers* by Frédéric Bazille (see Exhibit 2.1).[1] This piece depicts intensely lighted white, blue, red, and cream flowers in dark clay pots on a greenhouse floor. The resplendent, precisely detailed flower petals, contrasted with the dark green, less-detailed foliage and mere suggestion of flowerpots in the blurry, dark background, put the focus on the flowers. Through his expert use of color, form, and juxtaposition, Bazille conveys the vibrancy, brilliance, and softness of the flowers. Jim stared for a long time at this painting in admiration, since it conveyed to him the beautiful and joyful essence of flowers. This painting encapsulated the delight that flowers evoke with their vivid colors and soft, delicate textures.

Exhibit 2.1. Frédéric Bazille *Study of Flowers,* 1866. Oil on canvas. Private collection.

Later, Jim encountered another painting of flowers (see Exhibit 2.2). This painting, however, showed a consistently high level of detail not only for the flowers but also for the leaves, stems, vase, table, and wall in the background. Including the complete, com-

Exhibit 2.2. Frédéric Bazille *Flowers,* 1868. Oil on canvas. Private collection.

plexly detailed setting results in the flowers being small and therefore less prominent. The colors of the flowers appear duller and almost seem drab, so they don't stand out from the equally detailed background. There's no feeling of delicate, flowery softness. With the flowers, foliage, stems, and background painted with the same precise detail, there is no focus in the painting. The painting certainly didn't convey the same essence of flowers that the previous painting did, Jim felt, nor did it convey any sort of essence at all. While the previous painting had an emotional impact, this second one appeared decorative.

Jim glanced at the sign by the second painting, which was simply entitled *Flowers,* and was surprised to find that the artist was Bazille, the very same man who painted *Study of Flowers* that had so energized and inspired him a few minutes before. How could one artist paint such different paintings that were at extremes of inspiring and uninspiring? Jim thought that maybe the drab painting had been completed early in the artist's career before he had developed a mature style. However, the date for this lackluster painting was two years after that of the one Jim admired.

This was a conundrum: two paintings so different in style and dynamism by the same artist. Eventually, Jim located a book, *Frédéric Bazille: Prophet of Impressionism,* that explained their stylistic differences.[2] The paintings were, in fact, related. Following the exhibition of the first painting with the lustrous blossoms, *Study of Flowers,* at the 1868 Salon in Paris, J. Ixe criticized the work's haphazard composition and dark background in the *Journal de Montpellier* of May 25, 1868. Taking this to heart, Bazille painted the second, *Flowers,* with the flowers and setting in the same monotonous, high level of detail.

Thus, it seems Bazille created the two paintings for two different purposes. One purpose was, Jim hypothesized, to convey what flowers meant to Bazille. This resulted in the painting that captures the spirit of flowers. The other purpose, perhaps, was to show the flowers and their setting with technical realism. However, the painting that resulted from this second purpose is un-inspiring.

These two contrasting paintings by the same person emphasize the importance of understanding the essence of your offering if it's to engage your audience. To Jim, the essence of the first painting is the brilliance, color, softness, texture, and everything that makes flowers so bedazzling. The essence of the second painting seems to be to show the whole scene of flowers and their setting, and maybe to show off the artist's skills. However, this scene doesn't convey anything special to Jim.

This illustration of essence, we hope, will make it easier for you to understand the essences of products, services, and daily work.

Essence

Flair is effective if it enhances the emotional connection of cus-tomers to the product, service, or daily work. To do this, the flair needs to directly relate to the offering. If it doesn't, it's merely win-dow dressing that won't engage customers over the long term and won't create a buzz that spreads excitement.

To add flair that reflects the offering, it's necessary to consider the essence of the product or service. Some definitions of *essence* from the *Merriam-Webster Unabridged Collegiate Dictionary* are "the individual, real, or ultimate nature of a thing" and "the most significant element, quality, or aspect of a thing or person."[3] We propose that the essence of an offering can be viewed as: a concise, fundamental statement of what the offering does that reflects the customers' emotional and rational reactions to the offering.

To help us understand the essence of a product, let's consider the automobile. This is a straightforward example with which everyone should be familiar. The essence of a car is to get you from one place to another whenever you want, quickly and in your own space. This essence is in contrast to other means of getting from one place to another that have different properties, such as waiting for public transportation, summoning a taxi, walking, asking a friend for a ride, or not going.

A car manufacturer, however, needs to consider the essence of its particular car to differentiate it from other cars on the market. There are many attributes of the experience of driving and owning a car to consider that can help people differentiate one from another:

- the sensation of driving, hence people buy Porsches

- reliability, hence the popularity of Japanese cars with a reputation for dependability

- the price, hence cars can be bought for less than $15,000 (a Nissan Versa)[4] to more than $4,000,000 (a Lamborghini Veneno Roadster)[5]

- the cost of gas, hence people can buy a Scion iQ, which gets 37 mpg, or a Bentley Mulsanne, which gets 13 mpg[6]

- the number of passengers that can be accommodated, hence people can buy a Smart Car or a Lincoln Navigator SUV

Since people have varying tastes, different aspects of the driving experience appeal to different people. This is, of course, why so many car models are available. Once a car company selects the experience it wishes to provide, it can define an essence for its car offering. For the Lincoln Navigator, a statement of essence might be "large, luxurious, and well-appointed." For a Toyota Camry, the essence might be "mid-price, family-size, and reliable."

A Meaningful and Joyful Essence

We introduced essence as encapsulating what an offering enables customers to do along with their experience in using the offering, both considered at emotional and rational levels. It's also necessary to establish that the essence is *meaningful* – that people care about the offering. For example, many reviews of the first smartwatches offered in 2013 recommended against their purchase since they contained few useful (meaningful) features and applications. And it's also necessary to make sure that the essence is *joyful*, since people will purchase or use the offering if it brings them pleasure. For example, people buy BMWs for their exhilarating driving experience. There's a saying in marketing that people buy on emotion and justify their decision to buy rationally. Flair, based on a meaningful and joyful essence, touches both.

One of our favorite examples of an offering with a meaningful and joyful essence, which we've already mentioned, is the Apple iPod. Today you can play music on your smartphone, so iPods may not be as ubiquitous as they were in the early 2000s when they were first introduced, but back then they were a game-changer in how people experienced music. Jenn recalls the first time a friend showed her an iPod and how amazed she was to see her friend's entire CD collection in the palm of her hand – all labeled, organized, and ready to play. Within a few days Jenn purchased her own, and it was a constant companion in her purse and car. To us the essence of the iPod is "the joy of music is always with you." The iPod isn't just a device that provides music – it's a device that lets you enjoy music all the time, wherever you are. Jobs expressed this as, "A thousand songs in your pocket." But the word *essence* expresses the joy that the thousand songs bring you, rather than just the convenience of having them with you.

With this meaningful and joyful essence in mind, Apple designed the iPod to be simple to use so that it wouldn't interfere with experiencing the joy of music. Downloading music and assembling play lists was done on a computer that could handle this more complex task easily. Then the playlist was loaded onto the iPod to enjoy. Jobs understood that the essence of Apple products encapsulated both the joy of what the products provided (listening to music wherever you are) and the ease of how the customer experienced the products (assembling and playing playlists).

Now consider a case where the essence of the offering was neither meaningful nor joyful: Tropicana's orange juice carton redesign a few years back. Tropicana had long packaged its orange juice in a carton that featured a picture of an orange punctured with a straw, which sent the message that the juice was so fresh that it seemed to come directly from the orange. In 2009 Tropicana changed the carton's picture to a glass of orange juice. Tropicana's customers reacted negatively in letters, emails, telephone calls, blogs, and other media outlets.[7] The adverse reactions were of two types: (1) those who griped that the new labeling was unattractive and didn't make Tropicana seem special and (2) those who groused that Tropicana, without the unique picture of an orange, was now difficult to find on the grocery store shelf among all the other orange juice brands.

The essence of the original Tropicana offering featuring the distinctive picture of the orange and straw can be defined as "Tropicana is fresh." The best essence we can come up with for the changed packaging is the weak "Tropicana provides a glass of orange juice." The image change made some customers feel that Tropicana looked like a generic store brand, and this didn't make customers feel good about Tropicana. Not seeing the iconic orange pierced by a straw on the carton, some people complained that they went home with the wrong brand or with the wrong variety of Tropicana, since all the juice cartons looked virtually the same. It was definitely not joyful for customers to spend extra time looking for their desired carton of juice or to think that they were drinking a generic store brand when they preferred Tropicana. Tropicana orange juice sales dropped 20 percent between January 1 and February 22, 2009. To Tropicana's credit, the company listened to its customers and returned to the original carton design.

This example shows that, while Tropicana thought it was providing a contemporary update to its branding, there was no meaningful and joyful essence to the redesigned carton. And the redesign led to an unanticipated negative buying experience. In Chapter 11 we'll present ways to examine possible negative reactions to added flair to avoid problems such as the one Tropicana experienced.

Flair Can Apply to Any Aspect of an Offering

Flair can apply to the physical appearance of an offering, to what the offering provides, and to the experience of using the offering. The following examples illustrate a variety of ways in which an offering can engender a meaningful and joyful essence and, hence, many ways in which the offering can incorporate flair.

The brand Oxo took what was previously considered a rather mundane class of products, kitchen utensils, and enhanced the experience of using them. One of Oxo's first products was the potato peeler. Oxo increased the handle size and redesigned its shape to be more comfortable in one's hand. It also made the physical shape and color appealing. Oxo's insight was that the experience of using a potato peeler was as important as having the resulting peeled potato. Now, the essence of a potato peeler, obviously, is that it peels potatoes, and this is meaningful. However, a potato peeler's essence also includes the experience of using the peeler to peel the potato. Making the Oxo peeler comfortable to use gave it joy (well, as much joy as peeling potatoes can bring). Plus, the Oxo peeler now looks appealing, which is also part of the user experience. Oxo built on its understanding of user experience to create a thriving kitchen utensil business.

Another ordinary kitchen item made joyful is the Michael Graves teakettle with a whistling bird on the spout. Using the whistling bird teakettle to boil water is no easier than using other teakettles, so its function doesn't stand out. Other teakettles also whistle when the water boils, so its user experience of knowing when the water is boiling isn't special. The distinctive features of the Graves teakettle are the body's shape and bright finish, the handle design, and, most importantly, the brightly colored whistling bird on the spout – its physical appearance. Thus, the essence that provides flair is the appealing and whimsical design. Waiting for the water to boil is more pleasant when you look at the beautiful kettle and anticipate the whistle that will come from the bird. The essence of the Grave teakettle might be expressed as "be entertained while boiling water."

The Magic Castle Hotel in Hollywood, California, was originally a 1950s-era apartment building, and the building's exterior remains little changed from what it was back then. Jim grew up in Hollywood and Pasadena and has seen many Southern California 1950s apartment buildings that are lacking in physical flair. Most have plain, featureless stucco on the outside that's punctuated by windows with extremely narrow, characterless metal frames. These buildings were often built around a swimming pool in the center courtyard. Sometimes, balconies for the apartments that overlook the pool provide some visual interest inside the courtyard. So Jim expected to see a plain-looking, two- or three-story building when he and his wife, Joanne, arrived at the Magic Castle Hotel for a two-night stay in 2011. Indeed, the building exterior was every bit as plain as Jim expected.

Jim and Joanne entered the hotel, and as soon as the two staff members at the reception counter saw them, the flair of the Magic Castle Hotel began. These staff members presented big smiles and an enthusiastic, sincere welcome. As the registration process was being conducted with one of the staff members, another served chilled sparkling grapefruit juice in champagne flutes. They explained the features of the hotel: fresh breakfast pastries from the local Susina Bakery, coffee by Wolfgang Puck, ice water with chopped cumbers in a glistening glass dispenser, limitless free soft drinks and snacks, DVD players in the room with free movies, and arrangements that could be made to visit the Magic Castle next door that featured dinner and magic shows by magicians who are members of the Academy of Magical Arts. After settling in their room, Jim and Joanne went back to the reception desk to inquire about nearby sights and a restaurant for lunch. They received comprehensive and enthusiastic recommendations along with a map with locations marked by staff members. The recommended restaurant was wonderful. The front desk clerks' energetic, enthusiastic service and the limitless soft drinks and snacks were the highlights of the amenities. They even offered drinks and snacks for the road upon departure.

The Magic Castle Hotel took a plain, 1950s-era apartment building and turned it into a magical experience with flair for attentive service and generous amenities. The amenities weren't expensive but were special and unique. The essence of the Magic

Castle Hotel reflects Hollywood with happy, energetic service and fun amenities that convey the feeling of "show time." This flair certainly offset the bland architecture of the 1950s-era, converted apartment building. Jim would go back to the hotel anytime.

During the *Charlie Rose* television show on April 19, 2012, "We are glad to see you" was the expression that Charlie and Danny Mayer, CEO of Union Square Hospitality Group restaurants, agreed upon to capture the spirit of a great restaurant.[8] This seems to be a good motto for most any service, since it conveys sincerity and implies that all details of a customer's engagement with the service will be well executed. Furthermore, it implies that the service provider is invested in what it offers and is pleased to provide its services. We think, however, the restaurant could better express its meaningful and joyful essence by saying not only "We are glad to see you" but "We are glad to see you, and we want you to have a fabulous time."

Recently Jenn took a trip from Boston to Buffalo on JetBlue Airways; the amenities and service made the flight an enjoyable, easy, and economical travel experience. JetBlue began a decade and a half ago amid a profusion of well-established airlines, during a time when air travel seemed more like a necessary evil rather than a pleasant way to travel. Through such initiatives as low fares, engaging interior and exterior design schemes for their planes, personal televisions at each seat, and free snacks, JetBlue strives to make the flyer feel special and comfortable.

Unfortunately, Jenn's flight ended up delayed for two hours; but JetBlue handled this inconvenience with its usual flair – the next day they sent an email with a $50 credit for the inconvenience. Jenn has flown many airlines domestically and internationally, and long delays have been all too frequent. But JetBlue is the only airline that not only offered a credit but did so without being asked. This reinforces the feeling of flying with ease, convenience, and individual attention that is the essence of JetBlue. However, in February 2015 JetBlue replaced CEO David Barger, who was in charge when Jenn took that trip, with Robin Hayes.[9] Among the reasons for Barger's departure was his focus on passenger-friendly initiatives and charging few extra fees, practices that were considered to have raised expenses and lowered revenue. It will be interesting to see what effect having fewer passenger-friendly services will have on customer loyalty.

The final example in this section covers a briefing Jim gave to management during his time at the Volpe Center. Employees at the Center presented an overview of their work as part of weekly management meetings, where they described their work in technical terms. When Jim attended the meetings he got a general idea of their work, but he couldn't follow the details of their technical briefings. He was scheduled to present his work on project portfolio management and knowledge management. These topics were new to the Volpe Center employees, and no one in the audience was likely to be familiar with them. So Jim formulated a storyboard that explained the concepts, described the applications he was supporting with the clients, and showed why the work was important to the clients and the Volpe Center. He didn't discuss technical details of the projects. The briefing was the story, which could be understood by non-experts. It wasn't a typical technical briefing.

After the briefing Jim received many phone calls and emails from the attendees, who complimented him on his presentation and said that the format he used should be a model for talks at future management meetings. Jim concluded that the narrative format had engaged the audience in a way that strictly technical content wouldn't have. The audience was composed mainly of people with specialized engineering backgrounds, but they responded to a story with little technical content. The essence of the talk was "inform through storytelling."

Why a Meaningful and Joyful Essence Works

Oxford University Press has published a series of nearly 400 volumes of "Very Short Introductions" to various topics. One is *Happiness: A Very Short Introduction* by Daniel M. Hayborn, Associate Professor of Philosophy at Saint Louis University.[10] Hayborn states that there are five sources of happiness that researchers generally agree on: security, outlook, autonomy, relationships, and skilled and meaningful activity. The last source is relevant to adding flair by making the activity associated with your offering meaningful. Hayborn also uses the expression "worthwhile activities done well" to describe this source of happiness. "Activity matters," he says, "but not just any kind of activity. Passing one's day performing a mindless, pointless, repetitive task isn't one's idea of happiness. . . . The exercise of skill alone may have little impact on happiness if you don't see the activity as worthwhile or meaningful." Thus, meaningfulness can aid in bringing happiness.

Emotion: A Very Short Introduction by Dylan Evans, Research Officer in Evolutionary Robotics at the University of Bath, is another book in the series.[11] Evans says that most emotion researchers today accept that there are some basic innate and universal emotions among people, regardless of their cultural background, and that these include joy, distress, anger, fear, surprise, and disgust. Joy is the only emotion on this list that can be said to be unequivocally positive.

He postulates that joy evolved as a motivator to pursue a particular action. Joy as a motivator involves anticipation – the anticipation of feeling joy helps individuals decide what to do. Thus we conclude that adding flair, which is joyful, will influence a customer to buy and use your product or service and an audience to adopt your recommendations.

Evans states that joy and happiness aren't the same but are linked. He believes that joy occurs as a single episode that lasts only a minute or less, while happiness, which is a mood, lasts much longer. Joy can, however, lead to happiness. For example, Evans says, "The joy produced by witnessing a beautiful sunset lasts barely longer that the sunset itself, but the experience may put us in a happy mood that stays with us for hours." So flair, with its element of joy, can bring happiness that lasts after your offering is experienced.

What Job Will Your Offering Do, and What's Your Experience in Doing the Job?

Many business people are familiar with the job-to-be-done approach advocated by Clayton M. Christensen, Scott Cook, and Taddy Hall in their December 2005 *Harvard Business Review* article called, "Marketing Malpractice: The Cause and the Cure."[12] The job-to-be-done approach provides an alternative way to understand the concept of a meaningful and joyful essence.

The article advocates finding out what jobs customers want to get done and proposes that these jobs will point the way to purposeful products. The article quotes former Harvard Business School professor Theodore Levitt telling his students, "People don't want to buy a quarter-inch drill. They want a quarter-inch hole!"

Understanding the job the customer wants done provides a way to discover the offering's meaningful and joyful essence. Your offering needs to accomplish the job customers want done, but it also needs to do the job well enough to satisfy the customer. A hole that's splintery may be acceptable for stringing electrical wire inside the walls, but a splintery hole for a knob in a kitchen cabinet door isn't. If your offering does a job that a customer wants done and the results of the job are satisfactory, then you have a meaningful essence. If the results of the job are delightful, or at least satisfying, then you have a joyful outcome – the knob is straight and in a pleasing place on the door because of the well-drilled hole.

In addition to the result, the experience of doing the job is part of the essence, since this aspect also has an emotional impact. For example, if the job to be done is to create a hole, the process to make the hole can be easy or difficult, pleasant or unpleasant, depending on the ease of keeping the drill straight, whether the drill seems heavy or the trigger hard to pull, whether there's enough room to maneuver the tool, and whether there's sawdust to clean up. A tool that makes the job easy and pleasant is a tool that has flair.

The article by Christensen, Cook, and Hall mentions that every job people need or want has a functional, a social, and an emotional dimension. Examples of these attributes were discussed in a December 2013 webinar, "Customer Solutions Using Jobs to Be Done," presented by Innosight, a management consulting firm founded by Christensen and Mark W. Johnson.[13] The three dimensions were discussed from the perspective of the customer: functional is getting something done, such as drilling a quarter-inch hole; emotional concerns how the customer wants to feel in certain settings, such as feeling good that the hole was straight, clean, and easy to drill; and social is about how the customer wants to portray herself to others and be perceived by others, such as being seen as a competent carpenter.

These dimensions constitute another way to understand the meaningful and joyful essence of your offering. For example, people patronize an upscale restaurant for a fine meal (the functional dimension), to feel special because of its pleasant décor and attentive service (the emotional dimension), and to feel comfortable by interacting with friends or family (the social dimension). These dimensions cover the rational and emotional aspects to consider in defining an offering's meaningful and joyful essence. Depending on the specifics of how an upscale restaurant incorporates these dimensions, an essence might be, "dine on exotically flavored food, served by sociable and attentive waitstaff, while enjoying the company of friends and family in a festive setting," or "a formal dining experience of exquisite, classic French food in a formal setting with attentive yet unobtrusive service." These comprehensive essence statements might be boiled down to "festive, exotic dining" and "formal, exquisite, classic French dining."

. . .

In Part I you've learned the importance of meaningful and joyful essence in building effective flair. In Part II you'll be introduced to the six elements of flair, which are the building blocks for adding flair to your products, services, and daily work: story, entertainment, experience, sincerity, excellence, and energy.

Essentials: Understanding *Meaningful and Joyful Essence*

■ Your offering's essence is expressed through your customer's emotional and rational reactions to it.

■ A *meaningful* essence ensures that your customers care about your offering. A *joyful* essence brings pleasure that entices your customers to act on your offering.

■ Flair can apply to the physical appearance of your offering, to what the offering provides, and to the experience of using the offering.

PART II

The Six Elements of Effective Flair

Story Tell a story about your offering.

Entertainment Have your offering entertain your customers.

Experience Create pleasant, even happy, customer experiences.

Sincerity Construct flair to accurately reflect your offering.

Excellence Be sure your offering is high quality so it doesn't disappoint.

Energy Strive to energize your customers.

3

Story

Tell me the facts and I'll learn. Tell me the truth and I'll believe. But tell me a story and it will live in my heart forever.

— Native American proverb

OFFERINGS WITH EFFECTIVE FLAIR TELL A STORY. "How can you tell a story," asked Dominique Fillion, Reebok Sport Licensed Division Design Director, during our interview with him, "that can allow the consumer to have this emotional connection, or understand easily what you are trying to communicate, and motivates the consumer to purchase the product?"

Some time has passed since the design of automobiles conveyed a strong story of what an individual car represented. Today most cars have rounded bodies for streamlined airflow to save fuel, and they lack styling elements that would disturb this airflow or add weight. The consequence is that there's little individuality among most of today's cars. In the 1950s through 1970s, however, before

Exhibit 3.1. The Wide-Track essence of the 1959 Pontiac Bonneville is easy to see. Photo courtesy of Allen Watkin via Wikimedia Commons.

fuel economy was paramount, car designs often told a story about what a specific model represented.

The 1959 Pontiac was known as the Wide-Track, a slogan that captured the essence of the car. In his book *Glory Days: When Horsepower and Passion Ruled Detroit,* Jim Wangers describes Pontiac in the 1950s as being conservative, reliable, and dependable, but lacking excitement and fun.[1] Simon E. "Bunkie" Knudsen became head of General Motors' Pontiac Division at that time to revive it. With Knudsen at the helm, out came the 1959 Pontiac that had a new, wider width between the wheels, a look that conveyed performance and handling through its powerful stance (see Exhibit 3.1). Wangers says that it's believed that this new silhouette came about when designers mounted a wide 1959 prototype body on a 1958 chassis and the body hung out over the wheels, which looked ungainly. Knudsen instructed that the wheels be moved out to match the wider body. Thus, the Wide-Track Pontiac was born. This new, strong look caught on with customers because it conveyed stability and power and was immediately recognizable on the street. Wangers writes that the car "was literally a traveling ad selling itself." MacManus, John & Adams, Pontiac's advertising agency, came up with the term *Wide-Track,* which became the center of Pontiac's advertising and personified its brand during that era. The wide stance of the 1959 Pontiac told the story that the company was no longer a stodgy, predictable brand but rather one that effused power and excitement.

Storytelling in Business Today

Telling stories to pass on beliefs and events, to describe the human condition, and to entertain is universal around the world and existed before written language. Stories convey information in an enjoyable manner and make it memorable. Storytelling is intertwined with all forms of media, including books, journals, newspapers, movies, videos, and websites. It's part of most art forms, including theater, literature, dance, paintings, and sculpture. Storytelling is used in business, such as in advertising and in strategy statements, to help bring change and action to an organization. We'll trace some of these business applications of storytelling and then discuss how to incorporate effective storytelling into the design of products, services, and daily work.

Advertising is probably the most obvious place where businesses use storytelling. Narratives convey the advantages of using a product in a manner that connects emotionally with a customer. One of the first, and finest, examples of using a story in advertising is the mail-order ad, written by John Caples in 1926, with the headline, "They Laughed When I Sat Down at the Piano But When I Started to Play!~" (see Exhibit 3.2)[2] The ad's text describes the skepticism of friends at a party, pictured in the ad, when Jack began to play the piano. The friends' reactions then moved to amazement and applause as Jack played Beethoven's "Moonlight Sonata." The story finishes with Jack's friends clamoring to know how he learned to play the piano so well, and with Jack describing the correspondence course from the U.S. School of Music, where he learned to play. Scott DeLong, who runs the Viral Nova website that covers trending stories on the web,[3] is quoted by *Business Insider* as stating, "The ad doesn't just say 'Learn How To Play the Piano' or 'How To Learn Piano In 30 Days.' That's inherent in the headline. So it goes one step further and strikes into the human emotion that we're all selfish jerks who want to impress people. . . . We want to shock and surprise them. We want to feel on top of the world, and this ad promises your moment of glory all in just a few relevant words. That's why it works."[4] *Advertising Age* calls this arguably the 20th century's most successful results-oriented mail-order copy ad.[5] *Advertising Age* goes on to say that the ad "dramatically exemplified Caples' belief that people yearn to be carefree and popular."

Apple is a master at storytelling. Around 2007 the company ran a series of television ads that formed an on-going story that contrasted the Apple Mac computer as stylish and hip with a PC running Microsoft software as staid and conventional. Apple was represented as a young man in jeans and t-shirt (and sometimes a hoodie) and Microsoft as a conventional man in a sport coat and tie (and even a suit). Each commercial featured a conversation between the two men that contrasted the easy-to-use, fun, feature-rich Mac computer with a somewhat boring, up-tight, more lim-

February, 1927   *MONEY MAKING OPPORTUNITIES SECTION*

"Can he really play?" a girl whispered. "Heavens no!" Arthur exclaimed. "He never played a note in his life."

They Laughed When I Sat Down
At the Piano
But When I Started to Play!—

ARTHUR had just played "The Rosary." The room rang with applause. I decided that this would be a dramatic moment for me to make my debut. To the amazement of all my friends, I strode confidently over to the piano and sat down.

"Jack is up to his old tricks," somebody chuckled. The crowd laughed. They were all certain that I couldn't play a single note.

"Can he really play?" I heard a girl whisper to Arthur.

"Heavens, no!" Arthur exclaimed. "He never played a note in all his life. . . . But just you watch him. This is going to be good."

I decided to make the most of the situation. With mock dignity I drew out a silk handkerchief and lightly dusted off the piano keys. Then I rose and gave the revolving piano stool a quarter of a turn, just as I had seen an imitator of Paderewski do in a vaudeville sketch.

"What do you think of his execution?" called a voice from the rear.

"We're in favor of it!" came back the answer, and the crowd rocked with laughter.

Then I Started to Play

Instantly a tense silence fell on the guests. The laughter died on their lips as if by magic. I played through the first bars of Liszt's immortal Liebesträume. I heard gasps of amazement. My friends sat breathless—spellbound.

I played on and as I played I forgot the people around me. I forgot the hour, the place, the breathless listeners. The little world I lived in seemed to fade—seemed to grow dim—unreal. Only the music was real. Only the music and the visions it brought me. Visions as beautiful and as changing as the wind blown clouds and drifting moonlight, that long ago inspired the master com-

poser. It seemed as if the master musician himself were speaking to me—speaking through the medium of music—not in words but in chords. Not in sentences, but in exquisite melodies.

A Complete Triumph

As the last notes of the Liebesträume died away, the room resounded with a sudden roar of applause. I found myself surrounded by excited faces. How my friends carried on! Men shook my hand—wildly congratulated me—pounded me on the back in their enthusiasm! Everybody was exclaiming with delight—plying me with rapid questions. . . . "Jack! Why didn't you tell us you could play like that?" . . . "Where did you learn?"—"How long have you studied?"—"Who was your teacher?"

"I have never even seen my teacher," I replied. "And just a short while ago I couldn't play a note."

"Quit your kidding," laughed Arthur, himself an accomplished pianist. "You've been studying for years. I can tell."

"I have been studying only a short while," I insisted. "I decided to keep it a secret so that I could surprise all you folks."

Then I told them the whole story.

"Have you ever heard of the U. S. School of Music?" I asked.

A few of my friends nodded. "That's a correspondence school, isn't it?" they exclaimed.

"Exactly," I replied. "They have a new simplified method that can teach you to play any instrument by mail in just a few months."

How I Learned to Play Without a Teacher

And then I explained how for years I had longed to play the piano.

"It seems just a short while ago," I continued, "that I saw an interesting ad of the U. S. School of Music mentioning a new method of learning to play which only cost a few cents a day! The ad told how a woman had mastered the piano in her spare time at home—and without a teacher! Best of all, the wonderful new method she used, required no laborious scales—no heartless exercises—no tiresome practising. It sounded so convincing that I filled out the coupon requesting the Free Demonstration Lesson.

"The free book arrived promptly and I started in that very night to study the Demonstration Lesson. I was amazed to see how easy it was to play this new way. Then I sent for the course.

"When the course arrived I found it was just as the ad said—as easy as A. B. C.! And as the lessons continued they got easier and easier. Before I knew it I was playing all the pieces I liked best. Nothing stopped me. I could play ballads or classical numbers or jazz, all with equal ease. And I never did have any special talent for music."

* * * *

Play Any Instrument

You, too, can now teach yourself to be an accomplished musician—right at home—in half the usual time. You can't go wrong with this simple new method which has already shown almost half a million people how to play their favorite instruments. Forget that old-fashioned idea that you need special "talent." Just read the list of instruments in the panel, decide which one you want to play and the U. S. School will do the rest. And bear in mind no matter which instrument you choose, the cost in each case will be the same—just a few cents a day. No matter whether you are a mere beginner or already a good performer, you will be interested in learning about this new and wonderful method.

Send for Our Free Booklet and Demonstration Lesson

Thousands of successful students never dreamed they possessed musical ability until it was revealed to them by a remarkable "Musical Ability Test" which we send entirely without cost with our interesting free booklet.

If you are in earnest about wanting to play your favorite instrument—if you really want to gain happiness and increase your popularity. Send at once for the free booklet and Demonstration Lesson. No cost—no obligation. Right now we are making a Special offer for a limited number of new students. Sign and send the convenient coupon now—before it's too late to gain the benefits of this offer. Instruments supplied when needed, cash or credit. U. S. School of Music, 82 Brunswick Bldg., New York City.

Pick Your Instrument

Piano	Harmony and
Organ	Composition
Violin	Sight Singing
Drums and Ukulele	
Traps	Guitar
Mandolin	Hawaiian
Clarinet	Steel Guitar
Flute	Harp
Saxophone	Cornet
'Cello	Piccolo
Trombone	
Voice and Speech Culture	
Automatic Finger Control	
Piano Accordion	
Banjo (5-String, Plectrum and Tenor)	

Exhibit 3.2. In 1926 John Caples wrote what is now thought of as one of the finest examples of using a story in advertising.

ited PC. *Adweek* declared this series of "Get a Mac" commercials as the best advertising campaign of the first decade of the 21st century.[6] This series of ads formed a long-running narrative about the engaging advantages of a Mac over a PC, with each individual commercial being a chapter in the story.

Target's television ads tell the story of the joy its "cheap chic" offerings brings to customers. The storyline of a 2012 Target commercial, which is typically known as the Alouette commercial (since voices sing "Alouette" in the background), begins with a red balloon landing in a city, and colorfully dressed Target characters leap from the balloon's basket.[7] They run through apartments, houses, streets, and parks, turning drab furnishings and clothes into stylish, colorful decorations and outfits. The Target characters return to the balloon and rise into the air, their job of spreading joy by adding color and style done. Text at the end reads, "Color Changes Everything" and "Expect More Pay Less." The joy that Target's "cheap chic" brings to one's life is personalized by the narrative about homes and people brightened by Target.

Storytelling in business has expanded beyond advertising to spreading ideas and inspiring activities. Stephen Denning, in his 2001 book, *The Springboard: How Storytelling Ignites Action in Knowledge-Era Organizations,* describes telling stories to bring change and action to an organization.[8] Denning advocates telling stories that serve as examples of what can be done: what if an organization can act as in this story (he then tells the story) where beneficial action was achieved. He explains how, when he worked for the World Bank, he heard about a healthcare worker in Kamana, a small town in Zambia, who was trying to solve a problem in treating malaria in June 1995. The worker logged onto the website of the Centers for Disease Control and Prevention and found the answer, which was remarkable to Denning since in 1995 the web hadn't yet attained the status of a grand repository of searchable information. Subsequently, Denning realized that this story illustrated the benefits of the World Bank sharing knowledge among its far-flung employees. He went on to develop the concept of a "springboard" story that could ignite interest and action for change. Denning's storytelling, along with much of the storytelling covered in business literature, is about using narratives to explain and present ideas and strategies and to gain widespread acceptance within an organization.

These examples of storytelling in business show how stories personalize the message. Now we'll move beyond straightforward storytelling to show how to weave a story into the design of products, services, and daily work. Before delving into the nuts-and-bolts of story in offerings, however, we'll explain why storytelling is effective.

Why Stories Work

Stories have always been an integral part of human lives. Here are several reasons why they're effective in adding flair to products, services, and daily work.

- **People pay attention.** Jonathan Gottschall, in his book *The Storytelling Animal: How Stories Make Us Human,* asserts: "Human minds yield helplessly to the suction of story. No matter how hard we concentrate, no matter how deep we dig in our heels, we just can't resist the gravity of alternate worlds. . . . If the storyteller is skilled, he simply invades us and takes over. There is little we can do to resist, aside from abruptly clapping the book shut."[9] Now, this may be stated over-emphatically for storytelling in the commercial world, but it reflects how narratives that we put in an offering will capture the customer's attention.

- **Our minds fill in images and details.** A story conveys a sweeping visual of the facts rather than just a list of facts. Creating a story around the facts illustrates their use and value in a realistic context. Stories spur you to create images and fill in details that relate the story to your situation.[10] You can envision yourself using and enjoying an offering.

- **Stories teach and prepare us.** According to Gottschall, Steven Pinker's book *How the Mind Works* "argues that stories equip us with a mental file of dilemmas we might one day face, along with workable solutions."[11] Thus, a story about an offering can tell how it works, how it will deliver a benefit, and what experience it will provide.

- **Stories create a lasting bond.** Gottschall says, "Story, in other words, continues to fulfill its ancient function of binding society by reinforcing a set of common values and strengthening the ties of common culture. . . . Story is the grease and glue of society: by encouraging us to behave well, stories reduce social friction while uniting people around common values. Story homogenizes us; it makes us one."[12] Applying this idea to narratives about offerings implies that customers, colleagues, or audiences will have a common basis to share feelings about your offering through your story. They may imagine different scenarios for using your offering, but there will be a basis for dialog and for interactions to build enthusiasm.

- **You are motivated to act.** The book *Made to Stick: Why Some Ideas Take Hold and Others Come Unstuck,* by Chip Heath and Dan Heath, presents stories as one of six principles (along with simple, unexpected, concrete, credible, and emotional) that cause powerful ideas to gain acceptance.[13] The Heath brothers describe how the right stories encourage people to take action, since stories provide simulation (which they describe as knowledge about how to act) and inspiration (the motivation to act). People are more likely to act in response to an emotional message conveyed through a story.

A Good Story Well Told

In business you often want to convey facts, features, uses, and advantages of a product, service, or your daily work. Too often you tend to list and explain these properties. Stories are a more enjoyable and memorable way for your audience to absorb information than just seeing or hearing lists and descriptions. Stories provide the setting and context that are lacking in a simple list. Adding personal elements through storytelling creates realism that puts your offering within the actual life of the customer. The customer can then imagine how to use your offering and how it will benefit them. This personalization engages the customer emotionally as well as rationally.

Stefan Mumaw includes the use of storytelling in marketing in his book *Chasing the Monster Idea: The Marketer's Almanac for Predicting Idea Epicness.*[14] He emphasizes the following qualities of a good story: a well-defined, singular theme; clear characterization; well-developed plot; stylistically vivid narrative; dramatic telling; and audience-appropriate subject matter. Mumaw illustrates the use of these qualities in several advertising campaigns. One example he presents is the Nike television ads that show, not a specific product, but the drive of athletes, which reflects goals and desires we all have. This storyline encapsulates the Nike motto "Just Do It."

In business storytelling the narrative is intended to influence customers to act, such as purchasing a product, using a service, supporting an initiative, or making a business decision. To inspire such action with a compelling, well-told story, the first step is to understand the composition of your customers, how they might anticipate your offering, and how they might react. You want to express your unique vision, but in a way that will be understood by your customers and will create a desire in them. Considering who the customer is will help determine the amount of detail to include, the degree of specialized or technical language to use, historical references that might be included, and the sophistication of the story. You must also identify what action you desire from your customers, and what narrative content and structure will influence them to take that action.

Robert McKee is considered a guru of movie screenwriting.[15] His students have won 18 Academy Awards and 107 Emmy Awards. In his book, *Story: Substance, Structure, Style, and the Principles of Screen Writing*, McKee states that the writer needs to answer the following questions: "Who are these characters? What do they want? Why do they want? How do they go about getting it? What stops them? What are the consequences? Finding the answers to these grand questions and shaping them into story is our overwhelming creative task."[16] These questions can be adapted to business by changing their wording: Who are your customers? What do you want them to do with your product, service, or work result? What would influence them to do this? What might be their desires regarding your offering? What might stop them from pursuing your offering?

If the objective is for customers to make a purchase, then you must communicate what the product or service will do for them and how they will enjoy the purchase. Asking what will engage with customers emotionally is as important as asking what will influence them rationally. Considering the job the customer wants done, as we discussed at the end of Chapter 2, can be helpful here. Some story topics that will entice customers to take action are:

- What your offering does.
- The value of what it does.
- The ease with which it works.
- The joy it brings.

Addressing the self-interest of the customer is critical. In *Made to Stick*, the Heath brothers emphasize conveying worth to the customer when they quote Caples saying: "The most frequent reason for unsuccessful advertising is advertisers who are so full of their own accomplishments (the world's best seed!) that they forget to tell us why we should buy (the world's best lawn!)."[17]

During our interview in August 2014 with Boris Esterkes, Design Director of the adidas Sports Licensed Division, with whom Jenn worked for several years as an apparel technical designer, we discussed properties of a good story well told in the context of sports fashion design. Esterkes described the initial processes his teams use to build a design story that inspires a new product line. After defining the target customer and the essence of the garment collection to be designed, Esterkes gathers ideas to build and present a compelling story.

Esterkes described the necessity of using narratives to build brand value and create an emotional connection for the customer. This drives good design and increases sales. To develop and refine concepts for a storyline, the design team gathers and shares what's currently happening overall in the athletic apparel industry as well as in the design world in general. This process includes domestic and international travel to fashion-forward hot spots, visits to art and trade shows, analyses of other areas of trending design such as the auto and home furnishing industries, market research, and brainstorming sessions. From information gathered, patterns emerge as to where fashion design is heading in terms of colors, styles, graphics, and fabrics, and what design qualities are valued, such as sleek and simple or bold and intricate. A specific trend is then defined as the focus of the next design collection and merged with adidas's company ideals and current corporate message. There's also an emphasis on what's new and innovative and how this can be adapted to fit the brand. Thus, a story emerges that highlights the new product and strengthens brand loyalty at the same time.

Several Good Stories Well Told

The concept behind Pandora charm bracelets is one of the strongest contemporary examples of using story to sell a product. Originally launched in Copenhagen in 1982, Pandora expanded into North America in the early 2000s and became an immediate success through the immense popularity of its charm bracelet, as described by Mary Teresa Bitti in her article "How Pandora Jewellery Grew to Become a Mega Global Brand" on the *Financial Post* website.[18] According to Bitti, Pandora has some 10,000 retailers in 70 countries worldwide with 332 Pandora franchise stores in North

America, Central America, and the Caribbean. In 2011 Pandora sold more than one piece of jewelry each second.

Resonating most significantly among woman 25 to 49 years of age, the original charm bracelet (there are more choices available now) consists of a silver chord bracelet on which the wearer strings individually purchased charms that come in an array of colors, designs, and themes. Thus the owner can personalize her bracelet to make it unique and meaningful for her.

The charm section on Pandora's website boasts, "Pandora offers more than 600 sparkling charms in silver, gold, and two-tone. Find the perfect charm to represent life's special moments." And there you have the narrative – the charms are themed to mark a specific event, vacation, or family occasion that's special to the bracelet owner. Pandora found a way to link its product to the positive emotions and relationships that mark a person's life. In her article Bitti quotes manager of franchise development David Lamb as saying that Pandora is "a new look, affordable, interchangeable and it's all about life memories and unforgettable moments. Consumers love it." Marketing manager Keshia Holland, Bitti writes, says that "the beauty of the brand is that we encourage our consumers to share the personal stories and unforgettable moments that make life extraordinary. Our jewellery is designed to encourage the sharing of those stories with others."

Ikea, the popular, worldwide, home-furnishing brand known for being stylish and affordable, designs its store experience as a narrative, taking shoppers on a walking journey through each genre of housewares one after the other. After entering an Ikea store, the customer is guided along a set path – defined by the furniture display arrangements, a distinctively colored floor path, arrows on walls and floor, signs, and a steady flow of shoppers – that meanders through the store. This path tells the story of the Ikea offerings that are available.

Furniture, décor, and accessories are arranged in sample furnished rooms, showing how the items might be used to outfit customers' homes. In the corner of a casual family room, for instance, a sewing center is set up with a table, a sewing machine, a sewing kit, a chair, a light, and a bar on the wall behind with hooks for sewing accessories, such as scissors. All sewing items are for sale, even the sewing machine. One display room, with a sign saying that the room has 380 square feet, is furnished as a studio apartment with a living area, bed, kitchenette, and bathroom. Throughout the store, the products are shown in a way that conveys a practical use and creates an attractive, comfortable space. In her *Fortune* article, "How Ikea Took Over the World," Beth Kowitt mentions that shoppers are sometimes found napping in cozy-looking store displays – realistic scenes in a story of domestic life.[19]

Part of Ikea's strategy to reduce costs is to produce and order items in bulk, Kowitt states, so the same offerings are available at stores all over the world. To convey to shoppers in different countries, however, that the products they are viewing belong in their particular homes, Ikea does extensive research on each country in which it launches a store and adapts the displays to that culture. Kowitt describes how "the [display] rooms play an essential, if secret role, showing consumers how to fit Ikea pieces into their lives. Displays in Japan and Amsterdam could feature the same beds and cabinets, for example. But the Japanese version might incorporate tatami mats, and the Dutch room will have slanted ceilings, reflecting the local architecture. Beds in the United States, meanwhile, are covered with pillows." So not only does Ikea build a customer narrative into shopping experiences by guiding the customers along a set path through stylized living spaces, the company targets the story to specific markets.

Jim conducted a project for Kopin Corporation, headquartered in Westborough, Massachusetts. Kopin produces components and modules to build wearable headset products, such as miniature display screens and optics, voice recognition and noise cancellation capabilities, head gesture command capabilities, and thin, flexible batteries. In February 2014 Kopin launched its wearable headset components and held an open house for its new Wearable Technology Center in Santa Clara, California. The proposed invitation for the launch, drafted by a public relations firm, stated that the event featured a keynote address on wearable technology trends, a panel discussion, a tryout of Kopin's new wearable devices, and a tour of the Wearable Tech Center. Jim, in his consultant role, was asked to comment on the invitation as the invitees would perceive it. In reviewing the draft invitation Jim realized that the invitation listed activities in general terms but didn't present enough details for attendees to see what they would gain from the activities. There was little to motivate someone to attend. Jim rewrote the invitation as a chronological story of an attendee's participation at the launch event, beginning with the keynote speaker's subject matter; then a list of the panel members and what attendees would learn from them; followed by a description of the new wearable components that Kopin would introduce and how the attendees could give them a hands-on workout; and finally a list of the research projects to be showcased in the Wearable Tech Center tour. This story, written from the viewpoint of an attendee moving through the launch event's activities, conveyed what an attendee would gain from participating in the event. Now the invitation provided a narrative to inspire invitees to attend.

An example of analysis results in a narrative format comes from work performed for the Federal Aviation Administration by the Fort Hill Group, which is a small consulting firm started by Katie Berry and Michael Sawyer in 2011. Fort Hill Group specializes in human performance in complex systems, such as the performance of air traffic controllers and pilots in air traffic control systems. Early in 2012, the FAA asked the company to assemble a list of audio and visual alerts that computers in planned future air traffic control systems would produce to inform controllers that they need to consider taking some action. Berry and Sawyer designed a simple, two-page table in a story format that explained the purpose of each alert and the recommended response to the alert.

Down the table's left side were listed the multiple air traffic control projects being conducted by the FAA. Each alert pertinent to a project was listed by name under that particular project. Grouping the alerts by project lets FAA project managers easily find the alert information pertinent to their particular projects.

The story of each alert was told in the columns. The first column described the alert. The next column named the domain of operations to which an alert applied: airport surface, terminal airspace, or flying between airports. Other columns indicated whether the alert was related to safety or efficiency of operations, whether the alert was indicative of an actual situation or predicted a situation, the response by the controller to the alert, and finally the urgency of the alert (rated low, moderate, or high). The story format of the table told just about everything the FAA needed to know about each alert in an easily understood manner. Fort Hill Group's flair is evident in the clear, logical, and complete story told about each alert. In a recent email to Jim, Sawyer stated: "I certainly agree that adding flair to any project makes it much more likely to be successful. I'm always disappointed to see projects that are undervalued because the performer didn't clearly present the results in a way that engages the user. We make every effort to ensure that every customer-facing project we do has received the necessary design review."

Essentials: Story

- A story inspires an emotional connection to the offering.

- Possible story topics are:
  - What your offering does.
  - Value of what it does.
  - Ease with which it works.
  - Joy it brings.

- Questions to answer in composing your story:
  - Who are your customers?
  - What do you want them to do with the offering?
  - What would influence them to do this?
  - What might their desires be regarding the offering?
  - What might stop them from pursuing the offering?

- Address the self-interest of the customer – what's in it for them.

4

Entertainment

In entertainment we become committed to something – an idea, an image, a person, a product – by becoming caught up.

— Peter G. Stromberg, Professor of Anthropology, University of Tulsa

OFFERINGS WITH EFFECTIVE FLAIR ENTERTAIN. When Jim entered the classroom to hear a talk about the craft of composing powerful short narratives, the first thing he noticed was an electronic music keyboard on the table at the front of the room. One doesn't ordinarily see a musical instrument at a lecture on writing. Roy Peter Clark, the presenter for this session at the 16th Annual Narrative Journalism Conference in April 2014 at Boston University, began by stating that the way to teach a process is to slow the process, give names to and explain its parts, practice the process, then speed it up. To demonstrate this, he explained the basics of rock and roll, adding that he had been in a rock band when he was young. After playing a few notes, Clark said that the basic sound of rock and roll comes from playing the notes of a chord one at a time instead of together. He played a C major chord the normal way, with the C, E, and G notes played simultaneously. He then played these notes one at a time, from low to high, repeatedly. To Jim's amazement this continuous playing of C, E, and G *did* sound like rock music. Clark then explained several principles for writing powerful short narratives, broke each principle into parts, explained each part, and integrated the parts into a short narrative. Even today, over a year later, Jim remembers being entertained by the electric keyboard used to demonstrate the basic rock and roll sound. And he remembers the principles Clark presented on how to teach a process.

After explaining the above approach of breaking down a process, Clark used it to explain how to create a dramatic effect with sentence structure. Dramatic effect, he explained, is accomplished by putting the most important part of a sentence at the end, the second most important part at the beginning, and the rest in the middle. To illustrate this he wrote on a whiteboard a line from Shakespeare's *Macbeth*, "The queen, my Lord, is dead," spoken by Seyton to Macbeth.[1] Clark explained that *is dead* is the most important message in the sentence, *The queen* the second most important, and *my Lord* the least important. Then Clark wrote on the whiteboard the sentence, "The queen is dead, my Lord," and, "My Lord, the queen is dead." Neither of these two is as powerful as Shakespeare's original words. This simple sentence from Shakespeare, which was an entertaining example, has stayed with Jim as a reminder about ordering content in a sentence.

To demonstrate the effectiveness of putting a twist between the beginning and end of a sentence, Clark began again with his electronic keyboard. He played a C major chord, which sounded sweet and melodious. Then he played a C minor chord, which sounded distant and created tension (or "rub," in Clark's words). Returning to creating tension in writing, Clark quoted Mohammad Ali's words, "Float like a butterfly, sting like a bee," the television program name, *Buffy the Vampire Slayer,* and the shortest sentence in the Bible, "Jesus wept."[2] The dissonant chords and readily recognizable examples have also stuck with Jim to remember to apply a twist when looking to entertain.

You Get Caught Up When You're Entertained

The definitions of *entertainment* from the *Merriam-Webster Unabridged Collegiate Dictionary* are "amusement or diversion provided especially by performers" and "something diverting or engaging."[3] Peter G. Stromberg expands on this in his book, *Caught in Play: How Entertainment Works on You,* describing entertainment as an activity that provides pleasure.[4] Stromberg further states, "Entertainment is not just idle fun, but a social and cultural process through which values and commitments are generated." Thus, if a product, service, or daily work can be made entertaining, your customers will more likely become captivated by your offering. Entertainment inspires action, since people are more likely to follow through if they feel good or, better yet, excited about something. They're also more likely to remember content that entertains. The first definition above conveys that you, in a way, are a performer in providing flair for your customers, colleagues, and audiences.

Entertainment can come from watching an activity (looking at a whistling bird on the spout of a Grave's teapot), participating in an activity (using an iPhone), or being engaged in a social interaction within an activity (dealing with a knowledgeable, enthusiastic salesclerk).

Entertaining Flair

Entertainment can come from the way a product operates, the result of using the product, or the appearance and feel of the product. For a service, entertainment usually comes from experiencing the service. For work on the job, conveying the results of one's work in an entertaining way increases memorability and the likelihood the results will be used.

Visual Thesaurus, commercial online software from Thinkmap, provides visualizations of synonyms that are shown on branches emanating from the word you enter (see Exhibit 4.1).[5] Each branch presents synonyms grouped around a particular meaning of the word. The ends of the branches, in turn, branch out again with individual synonyms related to the meaning of the word in the higher-level branch. When *entertain* is entered into Visual Thesaurus, three branches quickly blossom to show three meanings: (1) to amuse or divert; (2) to maintain in one's mind a theory, thought, or feeling; and (3) to take into consideration or have in view. Then synonyms for each meaning sprout out from the ends of the three branches.

If you go to the *Merriam-Webster Unabridged Collegiate Thesaurus* website you'll find simple lists of synonyms and other words that are related to the different meanings of the word you entered.[6] Jim finds Visual Thesaurus and the Merriam-Webster thesaurus effective for finding a good synonym, but using Visual Thesaurus is certainly more fun. He also finds it faster to locate the appropriate grouping of synonyms with Visual Thesaurus. Clicking on a particular synonym quickly puts that word at the center of a new synonym diagram. The designers recognized that on a computer synonyms don't need to be displayed in vertically aligned paragraphs as is done in printed thesauruses. A computer display allows for a

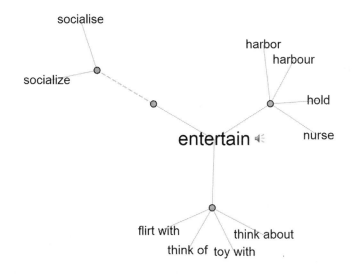

Exhibit 4.1. This Visual Thesaurus screen shot of a search for synonyms for the word *entertain* shows how entertainingly effective the tool can be. Image or text from the Visual Thesaurus (http://www.visualthesaurus.com), Copyright ©1998-2015 Thinkmap, Inc. All rights reserved.

variety of visual layouts, such as the nodal diagrams you'll find using Visual Thesaurus. And watching a display evolve on the screen is entertaining. Visual Thesaurus gets to the essence of what a thesaurus should do, and entertains.

Our family had lunch at the Seasons 52 restaurant in Burlington, Massachusetts, in August 2014. We were seeking a leisurely lunch with relaxed conversation. Seth (not his real name), our waiter, seemed to recognize that we desired an unhurried social experience and was attentive and open to short conversations about his work and the restaurant. We joked with him about humorous interpretations of the menu. We were seated next to the food-serving counter and were able to observe several intriguing dishes. Seth gladly answered our frequent questions about them. Other diners obviously were there for a quick lunch, and Seth met their needs as these other parties arrived after and departed before us.

Besides finding the interaction with Seth entertaining, the presentation of the food on the plates was intriguing. Some salads were served in large-diameter tall glasses and others in large, conical, martini-type glasses. A taco entre appeared with three tacos lined up end-to-end the length of a long narrow plate. Tasting desserts were served in small round clear glasses, much like large shot glasses, which added visual interest since the glass sides showed the desserts' layered ingredients. The dishes on the food service counter near us were fascinating in contents and presentation and were the subject of spirited conversation among us.

Seasons 52 entertained through the menu selections, shape of the plates, arrangement of food on the plates, visibility of the service counter displaying the fascinating food awaiting pickup, and small tasting desserts. And, more importantly, the food was good so the entertaining flair wasn't just window dressing. The entertainment from interacting with Seth came from his personality and serving style. But the style of the restaurant's food choices, presentation of the food on the plates, and overall atmosphere contributed to the amusing and leisurely interaction with our waiter. Seth felt comfortable chatting and kidding with us because the restaurant's festive style promoted this. Seasons 52 wants to be an entertaining restaurant, and it's achieved that goal.

Jim uses figurines that represent famous historical thinkers to emphasize points in his presentations. He sometimes gives workshops and talks about drawing from multiple disciplines to add flair to your daily work, especially in your presentations. To make his content memorable, he found foot-tall, plush figures from a company called

Exhibit 4.2. Little Thinkers can make for entertaining additions to your presentations.

The Unemployed Philosophers Guild to whimsically reinforce the different principles he covered. The Little Thinkers, as the company calls the figures, represent famous artists, writers, scientists, historical figures, and other well-known people (see Exhibit 4.2).

Some figures that Jim uses to bolster his points are: Socrates – to remember to continually ask probing questions when conducting work; Albert Einstein – to strive to create new concepts and understandings; Sherlock Holmes – to keep looking for facts and following threads to their conclusions; Sigmund Freud – to consider the human behavior aspects necessary for your recommendations to be successfully adopted and implemented; Charles Darwin – to continually evolve in your way of working; William Shakespeare – to write vividly; Vincent Van Gogh – to create amazing visuals for your presentations; and Charlie Chaplin – to add humor and entertainment to your presentations. Audiences have reacted with smiles, laughter, and interest when Jim shows the Little Thinkers.

As an apparel technical designer for Reebok, Jenn observed that design reviews, in which a new season's product line is presented internally, had the most audience involvement when the reviews were entertaining. Incorporating the audience into the presentation by engaging their senses brought new concepts to life and made clear the product's purpose. Dominique Fillion, Reebok Sports Licensed Division Design Director, told us that he likes to break up the monotony of design meetings to keep the team members excited and engaged. An effective way to start the meeting and introduce the story behind new designs is to show a video or blast music to capture everyone's attention and get them excited about what's to come. As Jenn can attest, these were not just YouTube clips being played for amusement. Designers spent hours scouring the Internet for video clips, images, and music that reflected the inspiration for their product lines and then edited them into short videos with relevant soundtracks to rev up the audience and set the scene for their design concepts. If a designer presented a retro-style hockey line of hoodies and t-shirts, for example, the video would show highlights from actual games played during that specific time period set to rock music from the same period.

Communicating initial design ideas that are largely in the designer's head rather than in a sample form is difficult, especially when many audience members come from analytical backgrounds. Concepts are subjective and design terms can mean different things to different people, so any props or items of reference help. Besides showing illustrations, photos, and videos, Fillion noted that tactile objects are often handed out throughout a design review. Swatches of fabric that will be used in the new garments, as well as previous seasons' clothing samples with a similar look, are passed around for participants to inspect and feel. If a retro hoodie is using a new brushed fleece, the audience can feel how soft it is and imagine a gently-worn favorite hoodie from that era. Sometimes a new graphic application is used for a team logo, so a sample garment using this technique, for example raised rubber print, will be available for people to handle to see the effect the designer is striving to achieve. Every prop and extra visual Fillion adds to a presentation is relevant and reflects the essence of the new product being shown. The added entertaining flair engages the audience and keeps their focus on the specific concept and storyline.

Essentials: Entertainment

- Entertainment amuses and engages.

- Entertainment helps customers be captivated by your offering, increases memorability, and inspires action.

- Entertainment can come from watching an activity, participating in an activity, or being engaged with others through an activity.

5

Experience

I hear and I forget.
I see and I remember.
I do and I understand.

— Confucius, philosopher

O FFERINGS WITH EFFECTIVE FLAIR CREATE AN EXPERIENCE. Jim likes to say that he purchased a new car because of his experience of pressing a turn signal lever. While exiting the Acura dealer's parking lot for a test drive, he pushed the turn signal lever down for the first time, and he instantly noticed the smooth action of the lever as it overcame the initial resistance, which indicated it was on, and the soft yet distinctive sound the turn signal flasher made. The turn signal flasher ticked pleasantly, in a mid-range tone that was just loud enough to indicate that it was on, without producing the harsh, annoying tick-tock that other cars often produce. Jim smiled and thought it was well-done – Acura was taking care of this small design detail. When exiting the car after returning to the dealer, Jim closed the door with moderate force to hear the sound it made, which was a reassuring, slightly muffled yet solid thud. The door handles outside and inside the car had an easy motion. Another pleasing component was the movement of the shift lever for the automatic transmission, which was easy to shift yet with a sure placement in each gear position. Jim's experience, or his "doing" as referred to in the Confucius quote above, with these small, polished details produced its intended effect on him. Jim purchased an Acura TSX.

Three years ago Jim dined at Bones steakhouse in Atlanta, Georgia, and was surprised when the waiter approached his table and addressed him as Mr. Poage. How did the waiter know his name, he wondered. The waiter then cordially introduced Bones and explained the menu. Jim discussed Bones's rib-eye steak and asked how it was aged, which the waiter expertly explained. The waiter continued to descriptively answer Jim's many questions about the side dishes, explaining the cook's trick for crisping the edges of the hash brown potatoes and describing the ingredients and preparation of the corn pudding. The waiter seemed to sense Jim's enthusiasm for these dishes and explained that the side dishes normally served two but that Jim could have a half order of each since he was alone. Throughout the meal the waiter maintained just the right level of attentiveness.

Other high-end steakhouses where Jim has dined have dark, wood-lined, heavy-feeling interiors that imply power dining and big deal making. But they're often overdone and pretentious and seem like stage sets for Wall Street tycoons rather than places for comfortable dining. Bones's wood-paneled interior was a medium dark tone that seemed appropriate to the hearty meat yet inviting as a setting to enjoy dining and socializing. The lighting also had the right tone and brightness for a classy, cozy atmosphere.

Jim's rib-eye steak was cooked exactly as ordered, the hash browns were crisp as requested, and the corn pudding's texture and flavor were just what he hoped for. Bones delivered a delightful experience with engaging service, inviting décor, and outstanding food. After accessing the Bones website for this book, Jim discovered that in 2014 Zagat ranked the restaurant as the best steakhouse in the country for both food and service. He certainly agrees with this ranking since Bones created an all-around exemplary and memorable experience for him.

The previous chapter presented another restaurant, Seasons 52 in Burlington, Massachusetts, as an example of being entertained. There is overlap between entertain and experience since one could say that being entertained is a pleasant experience and an experience can entertain. However, being entertained is more along the lines of being amused,[1] and experience is more about participating in events or activities.[2] While entertainment and experience may overlap, they are different paths to adding flair. At Seasons 52 the flair came from a festive menu selection; from an amusing interaction with the waiter; and from the edgy, sometimes whimsical presentation of the food. Combined, these traits created entertaining dining. At Bones the flair came from service that was knowledgeable, attentive, and detail-oriented; a décor comfortable for a steakhouse; and excellent food. Combined, these traits created an outstanding dining experience. These two restaurants applied flair in different ways to create delightful dining.

Why Creating an Experience Works

One of the definitions of *experience* in the *Merriam-Webster Unabridged Collegiate Dictionary* is "direct observation of or participation in events as a basis of knowledge."[3] Flair draws people in to observe or participate in – to experience – your offering. Another helpful definition is from *Keywords: A Vocabulary of Culture and Society* by Raymond Williams: "Experience . . . is then the fullest, most open, most active kind of consciousness, and it includes feeling as well as thought."[4] This definition encompasses the full emotional response a person might have to effective flair based on an experience.

Experience Expands Your Offering

The above definitions imply that: (1) rather than designing a product merely to accomplish a task or provide something, you should design the product so its use is also a pleasant experience; (2) rather than providing a service merely for the result, you should design the activities that comprise the service to also be enjoyable, both as individual experiences and when combined into an overall experience; and (3) rather than just presenting your work's findings, you should design your presentation of the work in such a way that your audience experiences what it's like to apply your results. Experience adds flair to your offering because it expands your designs to include the context within which the offering will be used and how your customers will react to it.

Experience Makes You Deal with All the Details

A common way to design an experience is to pretend that you're the customer and trace through the individual events that comprise your overall experience. We'll give an example of a grocery store, an industry not generally known for flair, and suggest ideas for all the touch points to build a food market with some dash.

Arriving at a grocery store, you'll turn your car into the parking lot and find a place to park. (An inviting arrival is provided with landscaping between the parking lot and the street, or with a brick walkway between parking lanes, such as at the Stop and Shop in Lexington, Massachusetts.) You'll then see the storefront and find the entrance – it shouldn't cost much to put color and a few architectural details on a storefront. Finding a grocery cart can be frustrating if carts are left outside in inclement weather or stored in a haphazard arrangement, but Market Basket in Burlington, Massachusetts, has the carts just inside the door where they're easy to reach and protected from the weather. Entering first into a floral department can bring a smile to your face, as in Trader Joe's in Burlington, Massachusetts, and Hannaford in Boothbay Harbor, Maine. Finding items on your grocery list is easy when the store has clear, complete signage and knowledgeable staff. Navigating through aisles is effortless when they're not blocked with pallets of goods. When you approach the checkout stations, a wide space for maneuvering your cart and accommodating lines makes access easy, and a short wait in line makes a shopping experience all the more pleasant. To exit the store, you appreciate a clear, wide path to the exit door and plenty of ramps from the sidewalk down to the parking lot. Lastly, you can breathe a sigh of relief if you can drive quickly out of a well-organized parking lot.

Sometimes a Good Experience is Simple

Thanks to Steve Jobs and Apple products, simplicity has become a key attribute of contemporary design. Walter Isaacson's biography of Jobs presents examples of Jobs's drive for simplicity throughout the book, and there is even a chapter entitled, "The Design: Real Artists Simplify," which quotes Jobs saying, "Let's make it simple. Really simple."[5] The book also quotes Apple's first brochure, which states, "Simplicity is the ultimate sophistication." Ken Segall has written a book called *Insanely Simple: The Obsession that Drives Apple's Success,* which states, "There's nothing subtle about Apple's love affair with Simplicity. It's everywhere you look. It's in the company's products, its ads, its internal organization, its stores, and its customer relationships. Inside Apple, Simplicity is a goal, a work style, and a measuring stick."[6] Jobs strove for simplicity in operation and physical design. For Jobs, simplicity helped make products easy to use, in part by making the design show how to use the product.[7]

Don't Make Me Think: A Common Sense Approach to Web Usability, a book by Steve Krug on website design, suggests that a common-sense approach to design is to make an item so easy to operate that users don't have to think.[8] Activities such as searching for information online may be candidates for flair, but the user may just want to get through the process quickly with little effort. Not having to think may not add joy, but it can avoid irritation, and that's joyful in itself. Any pleasure during a search comes from easily obtaining results. Krug's book addresses website design, but the don't-make-me-think theme can apply to other situations, such as smart devices, many software applications, locating a book in a library, driving an unfamiliar rental car, or finding a desired product online or in a store.

Sometimes Less Can Be Boring

The emphasis on simplicity implies that a design shouldn't interfere with a customer having a joyful experience. But this doesn't preclude adding details that make designs more meaningful and joyful. Adding appropriate and well-done detail can be effective in engaging people's interest and appreciation for a design.

Sometimes a detail that's unnecessary for function will enhance the user's experience in other ways. A prime example is the whistling bird that Graves placed on the spout of his teapots. This enhanced the user's visual experience. To determine whether to add a detail, ask yourself if it adds to the customer experience. Too many consumer products have an excess of features that engineers and designers find intriguing but that provide little value to customers. Details detract from the essence and cause confusion when they're added solely for flash or to raise prices.

Experience Flair

While she was at adidas, Jenn worked on performance apparel teams that designed and developed running and workout hoodies. A performance hoodie differs from a standard hoodie in the construction, fabric, and trim details incorporated into the garment. Instead of cotton sweatshirt material, a running hoodie will likely use a fabric with wicking action that pulls moisture away from the body to the surface of the fabric, where it can evaporate. The hood could have a "scuba" neck, which means it's raised an inch or two at the front to keep the neck warm, and the drawstring may have toggles to keep the opening tight around the face in windy weather. On women's performance hoodies, thumbholes are sometimes added in the cuffs as a trendy touch and to keep palms warm. If the hoodie is a zip-up, an extra piece of fabric, or "zipper garage," is looped over the top of the zipper at the neck so it won't rub against a runner's skin when it's closed. Reflective zipper tape and graphics can be applied to garments to increase a runner's visibility at night. Zippers are often added to pockets so keys can be sealed inside without fear of losing them on the trail. Finally, a recent touch is to build access for a smartphone or iPod into the garment by providing a sleeve pocket or a hole inside a main pocket to thread the earphones up inside to the wearer's ears. While these features generate a long list of added details, none add unnecessary complexity or detract from the essence of the garment. Each component is incorporated seamlessly into the whole and works to enhance the experience of wearing the performance hoodie for exercising.

Lyons/Zaremba, where Jenn had her first job after college, is a Boston-based exhibit design firm that specializes in aquariums, visitor centers, nature centers, and zoos. In the summer of 2014 Jenn and Jim interviewed Steve Lenox, the president, about how Lyons/Zaremba creates visitor experiences for the exhibit space it designs. Lenox described how Lyons/Zaremba's team begins with understanding the goals and objectives of the client and then evolves the design of the exhibit space to be responsive to these needs. General project objectives are to attract visitors, engage those visitors, communicate to and provide an experience for them, and ultimately transform how they think about the subject matter presented. Gone are the days of dioramas and explanatory signs, which create a less-than-thrilling experience. Lenox says that visitors passively looking at an exhibit isn't sufficient – he wants them to discover an exhibit's content through a presentation that produces a new understanding for them and provides an experience that becomes a part of their personal story that they later share with family and friends. The essence of Lyons/Zaremba's exhibit design philosophy might be characterized as creating a personal experience through the "joy of discovery."

Lyons/Zaremba has performed work for the U.S. Fish and Wildlife Service on its central interpretive nature center that serves several sanctuaries on Long Island. The nature center exhibit was intended to prepare visitors for a hands-on self-discovery experience when they enter a refuge – not just to provide facts about the area. Lyons/Zaremba and the client formulated the objective of the nature center: teach visitors how to spot and analyze evidence of different types of flora and fauna in the region. To meet these objectives, one strategy was to design a long table that contained a synthetic version of the ground in the sanctuary, with models of scattered logs, leaves, sticks, and rocks (see Exhibit 5.1). Visitors can move these items to see what's under them – worms, bugs, or other tiny creatures hidden from view in the real outdoors. Animal footprints were pressed into the fabricated mud to show what characteristics to look for, such as hooved, padded, or webbed feet, to determine what kind of animal left the tracks. Finally, visitors can discover some modeled animal droppings containing, say, fish scales, to provide clues to determine what type of animal might have left the scat. With fish scales in the droppings, the animal must be a carnivore that can catch fish, so it won't be tiny, like a chipmunk, but might be a raccoon, fox, or turtle. Elsewhere in the exhibit are drawers and cupboard doors that visitors can open to find more pieces of the Long Island wildlife puzzle. With different exhibits providing exploratory possibilities, visitors can constantly make new discoveries.

After experiencing the nature center, visitors can go outside into the refuge and put their newly found knowledge and nature skills to work. The overall experience of the nature center and refuge together provides the joy of discovery, changing how visitors think about nature in this region and encouraging them to create stories about their experience. Lenox refers to this transformative experience as the visitor taking ownership. The discoveries that visitors make become part of their own story.

The creation of art exhibits at the Museum of Fine Arts in Boston, Massachusetts, is another example of structured processes that provide an experience with flair. Several MFA departments

Exhibit 5.1. Discovery Table at the Long Island Complex Visitor Center at Wertheim National Wildlife Refuge. Photos by Michael Shackelford: Lyons/Zaremba Inc.

work jointly to develop exhibits appropriate for the museum as well as for museum-goers. We interviewed Chris Newth, Director of Curatorial Planning and Project Management, about how the museum defines the essence of its exhibits and goes about adding flair. While Lyons/Zaremba designs permanent exhibit areas for such facilities as nature centers, zoos, and aquariums, the MFA creates temporary and long-term exhibits featuring particular subjects and eras of fine art. When asked how he would define the essence of the MFA, Newth responded, "We use the word 'accessibility.' Our motto is that we want the art to be 'accessible to all.' That's actually in our mission statement. . . . We want anyone who comes in here to feel like they can understand it. Now, they may understand something, and that's different from what you understand. But then again they do not come in here and say, well, this is over my head, and I need to go." Catering to the general public, the MFA believes that everyone should have access to a meaningful experience at the MFA, so all exhibits, whether a permanent collection or a special exhibition, are designed to meet this objective.

To ensure that an exhibit is accessible to all, Newth explained, several departments work together to manage the various aspects of the visitor experience. He makes sure all team members are on the same page for the creation of an exhibit. The MFA's internal exhibit design department, taking the curator's thoughts and referenced artwork, designs the visitor flow through the gallery space, placement of wall art and pedestals, content of placards, and other exhibit elements. Flow through the exhibit, something appreciated but not necessarily noticed by patrons, is important. The exhibit designers consider how the visitors will know to go from one object to the next, how to tell the exhibit's story from beginning to end, and how to keep visitors engaged through the entire exhibit.

If any object is expected to be more prominent than others, more space is given for viewers to congregate.

Concurrently the education department focuses on who is targeted to attend the show and determines the best way to deliver the curator's message to that audience. The communications department entices audiences to visit the museum through advertising and media. Often the curators' initial concepts are too sophisticated, due to their extensive schooling and research on a given subject matter, for the general public. The communications department ensures that the exhibit's message is translated to reach a broad base of visitors. A key component in the creation process is that the mission statement of the MFA has been satisfied – all audiences must be able to acquire meaning from their exhibition experience.

To introduce visitors to the purpose of an exhibit, Newth said: "We have something called a curator statement at the beginning of each show. It's supposed to be a personal statement from the curator of what's going on here. Why did I choose this idea, and what do I hope you get from it. . . . It's supposed to be down to earth and [explain] what you're going to see. We have a Head of Interpretation who's charged with reviewing all text that goes in exhibit space. He also is the one who's trying to keep it simple and make it understandable."

One exhibit in particular that Newth recalled as a success, in terms of its public reception and visitor attendance, was *Samurai! Armor from the Ann and Gabriel Barbier-Mueller Collection,* which ran at the MFA from April 14 through August 4, 2013 (see Exhibit 5.2). According to the MFA website, the display of samurai armor, objects, and accessories gave the visitor a glimpse into the history and evolution of the era in which the samurai flourished.[9] In this

Exhibit 5.2. *Bagai* (horse armor), *bamen* (horse mask), and *bagu* (horse tack), Early-to-mid Edo period, 17th–18th century. *Tatehagidō* armor, Signed: *Takakage*, Early Edo period, 17th century. © The Ann & Gabriel Barbier-Mueller Museum, Dallas. Photo by Brad Flowers. Photograph courtesy Museum of Fine Arts, Boston.

case the collection already existed as a traveling exhibit that the MFA decided to bring to Boston when another special show fell through. Feeling that the displays and graphics that came with the traveling collection didn't match the MFA's needs, Newth and his team reformatted the visitor flow, exhibition layout, and informational placards to fit the MFA's aesthetic and mission to create an experience meaningful to the MFA and its visitors. The text provided with the exhibit didn't have the right technical and factual merit for the MFA, so the Head of Interpretation did a thorough rewrite.

Newth related the design of the samurai exhibit to the MFA's "accessible to all" motto by saying: "If you think of the samurai armor outfit, very complex, there are a lot of physical layers to it. We as scholars may want to talk about this little hinge developed at this time or made by this factory. But we have to remember that most of our visitors might want to just know how does it fit, what does it feel like when it's on. If there's a dragon, why is there a dragon on the helmet? Those types of questions as opposed to the really specialized. [It] doesn't mean you can't have the specialized; you just need to have a layer – what can the average visitor take away and get excited about? So I think 'accessible to all' is the right motto." Accessibility applies to everything, not just the exhibitions but also to gallery spaces, publications, and the museum website.

Samurais have a legendary and mystical aura, so the MFA designed the displays to create a visitor experience that was entertaining, educational, and awe-inspiring, no matter the museumgoer's age, demographic, or purpose in visiting.

When Jim gave a talk on a software program that was being developed by his previous employer, the Volpe Center, he created an experience for the audience as if they were using the program. The software was being developed for the Federal Aviation Administration to serve as an analysis tool to examine maintenance statistics of air traffic control equipment, such as radars, navigation aids, and instrument landing systems. The software is called National Airspace System Performance Analysis System. NASPAS analyzed such measures of performance as the percent of time equipment is operating (called availability), number of failures, number of periodic maintenance actions, and time required to repair or perform maintenance.

Jim was scheduled to talk about the features and status of NASPAS to managers from the FAA. Many technical talks that Jim has attended only covered the features of the technology. But instead of simply running through the capabilities of NASPAS, Jim decided to present the steps and results that might be used to conduct an analysis of a particular problem with the equipment. He created the experience of analyzing an equipment performance problem that began with looking at the number of failures of a sample navigation aid, then examined which model of this navigation aid equipment had the most problems, followed by the percent of problems due to different causes, and finally showed the number of failures for each individual location of the navigation aid model. With such an analysis the FAA could determine what model and locations of the navigation aid were having problems and needed attention. Jim performed the analysis in each of these steps before the talk so he didn't have to wait for the computer to process the analysis during the briefing. He presented the results in the above order to convey the experience of performing an actual analysis using NASPAS. At the same time, this briefing format demonstrated the software's capabilities.

The next morning Jim's supervisor conducted a review of the presentations that had been given to FAA managers the previous day. The supervisor praised Jim's presentation and said that it provided such a great start to the day that even if the other talks later that day hadn't been good, the day would have been a success.

Essentials: Experience

■ Experience is participation in or observation of events.

■ Creating an experience is achieved by designing a series of events that customers participate in or observe.

■ To create an experience, consider how a customer will interact with your offering.

■ Creating an experience makes you consider all the details.

6

Sincerity

The keys to brand success are self-definition, transparency, authenticity, and accountability.

— Simon Mainwaring, brand consultant

O FFERINGS WITH EFFECTIVE FLAIR ARE SINCERE. At one time or another you've been asked, "Was everything alright?" at the end of a meal in a restaurant. And once in a while there was a part of the meal that was disappointing. Have you ever replied that there was a problem? What was the reaction of the person who asked the question? Maybe they were flustered and didn't know what to say. They had probably been instructed by the management to ask if all was well but were never told what to do if the answer was, "No, there was a problem." In this case the question, "Was everything alright?" wasn't sincere.

One evening Jim and his family were asked the ubiquitous, "Was everything alright?" as they were leaving a restaurant on Cape Cod. Answering truthfully, Jim replied that the interior of the meatloaf had been cold. In response the cashier, who happened to be the manager, actually became angry with Jim for complaining, and the next party in line emphatically announced that everything was fine with their meal. Neither the manager nor the other customer took the question seriously. To them, it was more akin to asking, "How are you?" and expecting the automatic, and meaningless response "Fine."

Jim's use of the Little Thinker figures, described in Chapter 4, might be considered quirky, but it worked because the props were genuine. It's okay to try unusual ways to add flair if they're sincere to your offering. In fact, a unique twist to an otherwise routine presentation or offering can create a memorable experience if it's pertinent to the subject at hand.

What is Sincerity?

A definition of *sincere* in *Merriam-Webster Unabridged Collegiate Dictionary* is "marked by genuineness."[1] *Genuineness* is defined, in turn, as "sincerely and honestly felt or experienced."[2] Despite some circularity in these definitions, we conclude that flair is sincere if it creates an emotional response consistent with what the offering will do for the customer. It shouldn't just add window dressing in an attempt to capture attention in a flashy way.

Some business books and articles use the word *authentic* instead of *sincere*. Mumaw's book *Chasing the Monster Idea*, about characteristics of successful marketing ideas, has a chapter entitled, "Is it Authentic?" *Authentic* is defined as "conforming to an original so as to reproduce essential features."[3] We use the term *sincere* since the definition deals more with an emotional connection, which we deem useful in adding flair, but being authentic is also important, especially when discussing brand identity.

Being sincere by itself may not provide flair, but being insincere will certainly elicit a negative response. Flair needs to be sincere to work consistently over time, since the customers will tire of gimmicks and recognize tricks that are just designed to sell. Empty questions and pleasantries, such as "Is everything alright?" and "Have a nice day," are too frequently used to appear genuine. Furthermore, being asked, "Is everything alright?" is irritating when there is no plan for follow-up if everything isn't alright.

For a product or service, sincerity often goes beyond reflecting its intended purpose to convey the mission and brand ideals of the company that generated it. For example, consider the branding of adidas. The company has been using three stripes in a contrast color down the sleeves of tops, diagonally on sneakers, and down the legs of pants for decades and continues using this visual in new product launches to maintain brand awareness. While Jenn was employed by adidas, the idea of brand authenticity came up often in meetings, presentations, and reviews. All designers, developers, project managers, and other staff had access to corporate branding rules, and all products and marketing were carefully crafted to be authentic to adidas's message of excellence in sport and streetwear fashion.

Another company with powerful brand authenticity or sincerity is JetBlue Airways. Its design language is fresh and easy to spot, which enhances its image as an innovative, passenger-friendly, simple way to fly. Aboard the airplane, passengers are reminded continually that JetBlue strives to provide an upbeat and pleasing experience with its brand message carried through all aspects of the flight. Look out the window and you see unique, vibrant graphics covering the JetBlue aircraft, which stand apart from the other airlines with their similar, perhaps slightly dated, graphics. On the television screen in front of your seat the airline channel welcomes you aboard and wishes you a pleasant journey with that same blue hue and modern graphic design scheme. Like with adidas, all the brand elements consistently adhere to the same design language and are authentic to JetBlue's essence of cheerful, personalized flying. JetBlue even carries its branding identity into activities that involve only its employees. For example, whenever a JetBlue team works to establish service at a new destination, the employees talk internally about making that city a "blue city."

Sincere Flair

One of Jenn's most memorable projects from her time working with Boris Esterkes of adidas is the uniform design for the "Under the Lights" Notre Dame and University of Michigan football game on September 10, 2011, which commemorated the long-standing rivalry between the Fighting Irish and the Wolverines. The game's concept was to honor the heritage of these two dynamic institutions and their tradition of football excellence by outfitting the teams in new, high-tech adidas football uniforms with authentic retro graphics and styling.

Research is the usual first step in design projects, which Esterkes conducted by visiting the campuses, interviewing school officials, and gathering images of retro jerseys, school logos, game programs, photos, and banners. Then he fashioned a vintage look by blending the schools' throwback colors, logos, and attributes of their heritage onto the current, cutting-edge adidas uniform system.

An example of the fusion of school heritage with contemporary technology is how Michigan's M logo was designed and placed on the center chest of the jersey (see Exhibit 6.1). This yellow block letter was originally made from wool felt stitched to the jersey with thick navy decorative thread. For the "Under the Lights" game, ad-

Exhibit 6.1. Photo by adidas. Copyright 2011–15 adidas America, Inc. adidas, the 3-Bars logo and the 3-Stripes mark are registered trademarks of the adidas Group.

idas's new high-tech, stretchy, and lightweight seamless techfit jerseys were used, so a thick applied logo would have compromised the flexibility of the jersey and the player's movement. Instead, Esterkes used the M in the traditional block font and digitally drew a dashed navy line in the same pattern as the original stitching. The updated retro logo was printed as one graphic onto a pliable, lightweight fabric that was heat-applied to the techfit jersey. Esterkes added flair to these retro-inspired uniforms that was both sincere to adidas's reputation for using new technology to improve uniform performance and sincere to the heritage of these collegiate football powerhouses.

The sincerity of flair can be determined by examining the essence of your offering. A 2002 article in *Advertising Age* about branding described the effectiveness of Southwest Airlines's television ads that, at the time, used the slogan, "You are now free to move about the country."[4] This theme came from Southwest's examination of what it stands for, not just what it does: cheap fares that enable more people to fly to any destination. The tagline was an accurate reflection of Southwest's ideal of democratizing the skies by providing affordable air travel to all.

In the summer of 2014 Jim and Jenn attended the annual CEO roundtable discussion sponsored by the Harvard Business School Association of Boston. The panel included four CEOs from a variety of industries talking about "Building Leading Brands and Driving Growth." One of the panelists was Lizanne Kindler, who became CEO of Talbots in 2012 after the brand had been faltering in previous years. She discussed how Talbots had veered away from its decades-long aesthetic of conservative business wear targeting 45- to 65-year-old women in an attempt to capture a younger, trendier market. The clothing had been redesigned for the younger market, and the catalog had been updated, using younger models and showing a fit and style that didn't reflect the company's core customers. These misguided attempts to energize the brand and move in a new direction resulted in weak collections, a lack of cohesion, and a loss in sales. When Kindler took the helm she went back to basics and reinstated Talbots's classic look and brand identity. She emphasized that new styles are needed to keep up with popular fashion, but they must always reflect a consistent target market. A successful, long-lasting company must know who its customers are and maintain a stable brand message. So if you're adding flair to a new offering or service, make sure it's sincere to your corporate mission, as well as to the offering itself, or it may confuse and even alienate customers.

Project Runway is a reality television program on Lifetime in which fashion design contestants compete each week to create an outfit in a limited time following the week's theme. In each episode fashion experts serve as judges and choose a winning designer and a last-place designer, who is eliminated. The assignment for Episode 3 of Season 13, which first aired on August 7, 2014, was to design clothing that might be worn twenty years in the future. During the show Tim Gunn, who acts as a mentor to the design contestants and was formerly the chair of fashion design at Parsons School of Design in New York City, talked with contestant Emily Payne about the intent of her in-progress design. Emily presented her garment with a large hood that could be detached and turned into a purse. Gunn said the hood would have more sophistication if it just "is what it is" and would appear too gimmicky if it was turned into a purse.

Emily's final outfit was a short jacket with a cowl that couldn't be removed. While her design didn't win, it came in third out of fourteen. In this case the flair, turning the hood into a purse, would have been too gimmicky and not sincere to the design concept of the outfit.

In describing flair that's simply flashy and meaningless in its purpose, Jim likes to use the example of a businessman wearing a red suit to give a presentation. This would catch the audience's initial attention, for sure, but it would be distracting and perhaps even discredit him as a legitimate professional. Imagine Jim's surprise when he glimpsed a man in a red business suit gracing the cover of a *Financial Times* magazine. On closer inspection, Jim realized that this was a picture of the head of Ferrari surrounded by red Ferrari sports cars. In this case, a businessman in a red suit accurately reflected the offering being advertised and was sincere to the brand.

Essentials: Sincerity

■ Flair is sincere if it creates an emotional response that's consistent with what the offering will do for the customer.

■ Being sincere by itself may not provide flair, but being insincere will certainly elicit a negative response.

■ Flair needs to be sincere to work over time.

■ Avoid gimmicks that are not sincere to the design concept.

■ For products or services, sincerity also conveys the mission and brand ideals of the company.

7

Excellence

Desire is the key to motivation, but it's determination and commitment to an unrelenting pursuit of your goal – a commitment to excellence – that will enable you to attain the success you seek.

— Mario Andretti, racing driver

OFFERINGS WITH EFFECTIVE FLAIR EMBRACE EXCELLENCE. During a recent dinner at a Mexican restaurant in Boston, Jenn and a friend ordered guacamole that was made fresh at the table. Despite the high price this seemed a festive way to start a fun, casual dinner, and the waiters wheeling around tableside carts full of fragrant herbs and produce was the clincher. The server who prepared the guacamole did so with abundant flair, describing the ingredients as they were taken from individual bowls and mixed in a large, stone serving basin. The spirited preparation not only entertained but also built anticipation of tasting a fantastic guacamole. But what a letdown when Jenn and her friend finally tasted the dish. It was terrible – bland and incredibly sweet. Jenn now considers the restaurant a bad choice no matter what she might order or how fabulous the service might be.

What happened here? The experience, as a whole, was a failure since the flair of being entertained produced a bad result. Flair isn't effective if its outcome isn't excellent.

We've discussed how the first four elements of flair contribute to a successful offering. But the importance of excellence can't be overstated. If an offering is poorly done, or if the results of using the offering disappoint, no amount of flair based on the other elements will compensate. Lack of excellence just irritates. In fact, excellence itself can energize and be considered flair.

There are three aspects of excellence we need to consider: excellence in the offering itself, excellence in the results of using the offering, and excellence extending throughout the offering. Any offering can have more than one of these aspects.

Excellence in an Offering Itself

Apple is a prime example of a company that produces excellent offerings. Not only is the visual design of the iPhone sleek, minimalistic, and iconic, but the physical material and construction of the product are of stellar quality. The iPhone feels comfortable in the hand, and the display of content on the screen is attractively designed. Moreover, the operation of Apple products is excellent. Navigation is quick and easy.

The market share dominance of Google's search engine is based on the excellence of its search algorithms. The home page for Google is clean and basic, without the clutter of news headlines, weather, and ads, so the user can focus and get down to the business of searching without distraction. Sometimes the word *Google* is shown in colorful designs or animations representing a holiday, someone's birthday, or an important event, providing a bit of whimsy. Mostly, though, the website is about conducting a fast, first-rate search. Focusing narrowly on search excellence works for Google.

Both Apple and Google, besides demonstrating excellence in the appearance and operation of their offerings, have displayed excellence in the results of their offerings. Thus, Apple and Google are examples of providing the three aspects of excellence: in the offering itself, the use of the offering, and throughout the offering.

The smartwatches that appeared a few years ago were initially criticized for being unattractive. Recent smartwatches, however, have been revamped and now receive positive reviews for appearance. In reviewing the Sony SmartWatch 2 in the January 10, 2014, edition of the *Financial Times's* Paul Taylor said, "The SmartWatch 2, launched late last year, fuses high tech with high fashion. It would look perfectly at home on a fashion show walkway or in a board-room with its black metallic case, single stainless steel on/off button, and square glass display."[1] In his review of the Samsung Galaxy Gear smartwatch in a *New York Times* article from October 2014, David Pogue wrote, "The watch is huge, but it's beautifully disguised to hide its hugeness. You can buy it with a plastic wristband in different colors."[2] Jody Rosen, *The New York Times Style Magazine's* critic at large, said about the Apple Watch: "It's a lovely thing; as a watch, a plain old watch, I like it a lot. It has an 'Ion-X Glass' screen that is nestled inside a 42-millimeter silver aluminum case and a snazzy powder-blue watchband made of very comfortable fluoroelastomer rubber. . . . I'm partial to the sleek 'Modular' look, which I've customized to display the time of day, the weather and the 'moon phase,' mostly because I like to glance at my wrist and see Apple's pretty little rendering of the moon, floating in the starless sky of the Retina display screen."[3]

However, smartwatches haven't fully reached excellence in their operation. Pogue, continuing on about Samsung's smartwatch, said, "And Samsung, sooner or later, will learn that it can't build a coherent device just by throwing features at it. The Gear is a human-interface train wreck. All of it. The software design, user guide, English translations, and design consistency." Farhad Manjoo, reporting on wearing the Apple Watch for a week, gave a mixed opinion in *The New York Times*: "If all this sounds complicated, you're right. It is slightly difficult to get the hang of the Apple Watch, at least at first. . . . It took me at least a day to feel confident at shuttling around the different parts of the watch. Since it's a brand-new device, it stands to reason there will be a bit of a learning curve involved. Still, the Apple Watch presents an uncharacteristic first impression, one that many may find daunting."

Excellence in the Results of Using an Offering

Reviewers of the recent smartwatches vary as to whether they think the watches provide excellent results. Taylor went on to write in his Sony SmartWatch 2 review, "Most [smartwatches], including the SmartWatch 2, function simply as wrist-based mini-screens relaying information from a host smartphone. Nice to have, but until they do more I'm not sure they are worth the $200 that most currently cost, including the SmartWatch 2." Writing about Samsung's smartwatch, Pogue said "Let's admit it: that is an absolutely unbelievable list of features for a watch. If you'd showed this to someone in 1980, they would have fallen down and worshiped you as a god. But just throwing a bunch of trees into a pit doesn't make it a log cabin." Hiawatha Bray wrote a mixed review of the Apple Watch in *The Boston*

Globe: "This thing's going to sell in the millions. It will be the first smartwatch to become a full-fledged mass-market hit. And I'm not buying one. Because cool as it is, I really don't need one." Manjoo also gave a mixed opinion at the end of his article in *The New York Times:* "The watch, for now, is all business, aimed solely at improving your productivity. For some users, that alone might be worth several hundred dollars." So as trendy or innovative as these devices may be, their lack of excellence across a broad, robust range of useful capabilities detracts from their universal appeal to consumers.

New technology allows for the enhancement of excellence in the service industry as well as in product design. The entertainment industry is always looking for new and better ways to capture attention, and a popular service today is streaming media, available through sites such as Netflix and Amazon.com. Trent Hamm wrote online for *The Simple Dollar* in September 2014, "[Netflix] has over ten million customers, brings in $2 billion in revenue a year, and has had their stock go up 550 percent since the [2002] IPO."[4] Their success, Hamm postulates, is due to a lively, positive corporate culture and having "one of the best customer service ratings of any retail corporation in America." Of course, where success in retail is concerned, good service alone isn't enough – the product must be stellar as well. As streaming shows for binge watching has become a popular past-time, Netflix presents whole seasons, or even entire series, for customers to indulge in for hours at a time or one-by-one whenever it suits them. Another large pull for Netflix has come through the original series the company produces and streams exclusively on its site. The Netflix original shows "House of Cards" and "Orange is the New Black" have both been nominated for and won awards, and they have enormous audience followings. Not only do these extremely well-done original series increase membership in Netflix, they bring notoriety to the company. Steel quotes Keith LeGoy, president of international distribution at Sony Pictures Television, saying, "there are lots and lots and lots and lots of [streaming services,]" but "Netflix is the one that everybody speaks about."

For an example of excellence in one's work efforts (actually coming up short of excellence), consider a talk Jim heard that was presented by a consulting organization to the FAA's Air Traffic Control System Command Center in northern Virginia. The System Command Center monitors and manages the flow of aircraft throughout the country. It coordinates solutions at a national level for weather impacts and airport congestion in order to minimize delays. During the talk, charts were presented to show how air traffic was growing again after its decline following 9/11. The information on trends in daily flights, flights by type of day, delays, and cancellations was compelling, and the charts were clear and easily understandable. Through this skillfully illustrated format, the talk held interest. Jim realized by the end, however, that the information didn't address any decision-making aspects for managing air traffic. It left little to follow up on. A successful work-related talk would not only have excellent presentation flair to draw interest and be understandable, it would also be designed to serve a purpose for the audience.

Excellence Extending throughout an Offering

Jim finds the Fiat 500 to be the best-looking small car on the road. For an inexpensive car, it has a stylish exterior and a snappy interior – Italian car companies do know how to do style. "Its cuteness is undeniable, inside and out," said Emiliana Sandoval in *Motor Trend* magazine, "and it earned many a thumbs-up from strangers. I love the simple, retro/modern dash design, a nice expression of the Fiat's Italian genes."[5] Edmunds.com referred to the Fiat 500 as having, "Distinctive styling . . . perky, fun-loving styling."[6] While in Santa Barbara, California, Jim was intrigued by a Fiat that caught his eye with its handsome and elegant appearance. He talked to the owners, who spoke glowingly of its wonderful design – they had the "500 by Gucci" designer edition that was available in 2012 and 2013. They said that it handled well for an inexpensive car. Although the car has a well-designed appearance, the reliability ratings for the Fiat 500 aren't stellar, and so Jim hasn't purchased one.[7,8] Flair in appearance and performance may not be sufficient if excellence doesn't encompass the whole package.

The Spanish clothing label Zara employs a unique business model that has enabled it to dominate its target market: fashion-conscience shoppers aged 18 to 40 with mid-level income. Zara's flair comes from offering inexpensive, extremely fashion-forward pieces that reflect the latest styles seen in fashion shows and on the street. In 2010, according to Tobias Buck in his 2014 *Financial Times* article, "A Better Business Model," Inditex, the company that owns Zara, surpassed Gap in sales to become the largest clothing retailer in the world.[9] For a decade Zara opened one store a day throughout the world, Buck states.

The traditional business model for apparel companies uses an 18-month cycle, approximately, from design through delivery of new products. Once designs are created at the company, they're sent overseas to have samples made and then sent back to the design office to be reviewed and revised. This process is repeated several times. Garments that sell well are carried over into the next season, perhaps with a color change. Large batches of product are ordered to save money, which leads to discount sales on lingering inventory.

Pablo Isla, Inditex's chairman and chief executive, is quoted by Buck as saying, "Instead of designing a collection long before the season, and then working out whether clients like it or not, we try to understand what our customers like, and then we design it and produce it." Buck describes how Zara takes a new garment from design to sales in as little as two weeks. Customer feedback is obtained in stores by sales associates so designers can combine it instantaneously with changing trends and their own ideas. Buck reports, "Every day, tens of thousands of customer reactions are fed back to the design teams. Is the sleeve too tight? Are the fringes too long? Does your bottom look big in this? The answers are analyzed and swiftly incorporated into new designs, creating a never-ending cycle of iteration and innovation." To save weeks or months of time communicating and sending items overseas, cutting and sewing of samples is done in-house, and production is done locally or in nearby countries. This fast product turn-around and direct feedback system allows Zara to capture trends as they hit the high-fashion scene and give customers what they want early. Unlike its competitors, small production runs keep Zara's inventory low so it can offer current trends, quickly move on to the next trend, and make adjustments requested by consumers. Shipments of new inventory to the stores are made twice a week, four or five times more frequently than most retailers.

The excellence of Zara's offering is clear: selling on-trend items at a low cost. It's a result of excellence in its internal processes: quick turn-around and fast incorporation of constant customer feedback. This flair of bringing fast-fashion to hip, young, middle-income consumers is made possible through quick analysis of the market and an untraditional business model.

As mentioned in the last chapter, the television show *Project Runway* showcases aspiring fashion designers who are judged each week on an original outfit they design and construct. The experts judge each design on whether it reflects the week's theme, whether it's unique, and whether someone would wear it. But they also consider its construction – the excellence of the execution. A dress design might awe the judges on the runway, but if it fits poorly, has puckering at the seams, or presents a sloppy hem, it will be deemed unwearable. The judges (and customers) look at the whole package.

Essentials: Excellence

■ Flair isn't effective if its outcome isn't excellent.

■ Lack of excellence irritates customers.

■ Excellence itself can energize and be considered flair.

■ Three aspects of excellence are:

- Excellence in the offering itself

- Excellence in the results of using the offering

- Excellence extending throughout the offering

8

Energy

Enthusiasm finds the opportunities and energy makes the most of them.

— Kay Redfield Jamison, Professor of Psychiatry, Johns Hopkins University School of Medicine

OFFERINGS WITH EFFECTIVE FLAIR ENERGIZE CUSTOMERS. Hundreds, reported Nancy Luna in *The Orange County Register* in 2011, came to purchase burgers at the opening of a new In-N-Out Burger in Allen, Texas.[1] Customers camped out beginning at 4:00 p.m. the day before the opening, and the line of waiting patrons wrapped around the building. One customer drove forty-five miles to eat a burger on opening day. A refrigerated truck in the parking lot continuously replenished the restaurant's supplies. An In-N-Out "All Star" crew of veteran employees, who help new stores deal with the crowds at openings, oversaw operations at the restaurant for the first few weeks.[2]

The burgers at In-N-Out are always made with fresh ingredients, are made-to-order, and don't ever sit under a warming lamp. Meat patties are never frozen. They're fried on the grill when ordered. Tomatoes are sliced, lettuce is hand-leafed, and potatoes are peeled and sliced as needed. In-N-Out has a secret menu – although it's not so secret these days since it's on the In-N-Out website as the "Not-So-Secret Menu" – of such items as a Protein Style burger, where the burger comes wrapped in lettuce instead of a bun, and Animal Style fries, which come with melted cheese, grilled onions, and In-N-Out sauce.[3] The always fresh, tasty burgers and fries form the flair at In-N-Out Burger that energized hundreds of fans to wait for hours at the Allen opening.

Energy Evokes Action and Spreads the Message

An offering that delights you is more likely to invigorate you to take an action, such as purchasing a product, using a service, or implementing recommendations at work. For example, a car that drives around corners without leaning is much more energizing for the driver than a car that must be slowed down before cornering. A well-prepared meal, an artistic presentation on intriguing plates, and friendly, engaging service will energize you to revisit a restaurant and may inspire you to leave a generous tip. You're likely to feel energized after a briefing at work when you clearly understand how the recommendations will create value, as opposed to just viewing a bunch of charts that convey facts.

A definition of *energy* in the *Merriam-Webster Unabridged Collegiate Dictionary* is useful for discussing flair: "the capacity of acting or being active."[4] This definition implies that a person who is energized is likely to act. Being energized about an offering is akin to having a positive emotional response to the offering, a concept frequently cited as an objective of marketing. Mumaw's book

Chasing the Monster Idea has a chapter entitled "Does it evoke an emotional response?" In *Made to Stick,* one of the Heath brothers' principles for an idea to gain traction is emotion, on which they expand in a chapter simply entitled "Emotional." These authors stress the importance of building an emotional connection between the consumer and an offering.

Kay Redfield Jamison states in her book *Exuberance: The Passion for Life* that exuberance primes people to act.[5] It raises mental and physical energies and helps override inhibitions that block action. Jamison goes on to quote C. S. Lewis from his book *Mere Christianity:* "If you want to get warm you must stand near the fire: if you want to get wet you must get into the water. If you want joy, power, peace, eternal life, you must get close to, or even into, the thing that has them. . . . If you are close to it, the spray will wet you: if you are not, you will remain dry." If your offering brings joy and energy, people will act to use it.

Jamison, furthermore, declares that exuberance is contagious and helps to disperse emotion throughout a group. As she puts it, "The quick dispersal of exuberant or triumphant emotion accelerates the spread of the news of victory, opportunity in the environment, a new idea. It sends the message that it is time to explore, to gather as a group, to celebrate, to have fun. When there is cause for celebration, or collective enthusiasm and energy are required, infectious fervor will further a swift dissemination." Energy thus moves, spreads, and propels the popularity of an offering. Enthusiastic customers talk about it and share their excitement with others. Services or products that energize are poised for mass appeal.

Rob Cross, Wayne Baker, and Andrew Parker published the article "What Creates Energy in Organizations?" in the Summer

2003 issue of *Sloan Management Review*.[6] This article talks about how a person may be known as an energizer, someone who can spark progress on projects or within groups. Energizers are more likely to have their ideas considered and put into action. Some people, on the other hand, seem to be de-energizers, who drain the life out of a meeting and the people they meet. They can even negatively affect the productivity of people they might not even know. Adding flair to your work can make you an energizer, and you will likely be seen as inspiring others, performing better, sparking better morale, and worth being sought after for projects and teams.

Energizing Customers, Colleagues, and Audiences

Apple once again provides an example for effective flair, this time for exciting customers. So much enthusiasm is generated around Apple products that customers line up outside stores, and even camp out all night, to be among the first purchasers of new devices. On the day the Apple iPhone 6 first went on sale there were several online postings noting that crowds had gathered the night before to purchase the phone the next morning. Geoff Herbert, in *Syracuse.com,* reported that fifteen customers were waiting outside the Apple Store at the Destiny USA shopping mall in Syracuse, New York, the evening prior to the iPhone 6 release.[7] Workers cordoned off an area for the dozens of others who were expected to arrive overnight and in the early morning. At Boston's Back Bay Apple store, before its 8:00 a.m. opening, hundreds waited in a line that wrapped around the block, reported Hiawatha Bray and Taryn Luna in the *Boston Globe*.[8] The crowds gathered not for the launch of a new device, but for the seventh upgrade of the iPhone. In fact, each upgrade after the iPhone 3GS, introduced in 2009, sold more than the previous version during the first weekend it was offered.

Energizing customers through hype and a unique offering is illustrated by the opening of the first New England location of Sonic in Peabody, Massachusetts, in 2009. Jonathan Phelps's Boston Globe article on September 9, 2009, described the allure of Sonic's successful Peabody opening.[9] The 1950s-style fast food chain is known for its drive-in service, vintage charm, and menu of classic American snack foods such as loaded Coney hot dogs, Sonic burgers, and tater tots.[10] As Phelps wrote, "It [is] reminiscent of the 1950s, the glory days of drive-ins: carhops on roller skates carrying burgers and shakes, lots of tailgating, and the aroma of fries wafting through the air." Prior to opening a New England location, Sonic ran national television ad campaigns so Massachusetts locals were privy to its food options and fun atmosphere even though they could not yet get to a local Sonic. Even before the opening, the chain's name became known and associated with its nostalgic charm, and excitement was created for the opening.

For several weeks after opening, customers waited for up to four hours to park at the drive-in, Phelps stated, causing frequent late-night traffic jams. Although it was in an area saturated with fast food chains, Sonic attracted an estimated 54,000 customers in its first ten days. Phelps went on to write that the restaurant "has been so popular in Peabody that the owners have hired a valet company to direct cars into the drive-in and a police detail to manage the traffic flow." Phelps quoted Gina and Gregg Manasterio, the franchise owners, as attributing the initial success of their Sonic opening to strong brand growth and a unique concept.

Jim heard Edward Tufte give a one-day course on "Presenting Data and Information" a dozen years or so ago in Boston. Attendance at the course numbered several hundred, which was the largest crowd for a training course Jim has ever experienced in his 40-year career. Tufte is a guru in data visualization and has written four books, which have sold nearly two million copies, on the subject. His flair is the clear, unique, intriguing way he presents data visually. Added to this is the way he shares his techniques – through the quality of his writing and through the entertaining way he conducts his one-day courses. At the course Jim attended, Tufte had a magician perform to illustrate how large displays can hide small displays. Tufte presented examples of data displays that helped explain the 1986 Challenger launch decision, Charles Joseph Minard's map of Napoleon's march into and retreat from Russia in 1812, and the acquittal of organized crime boss John Gotti in 1987. Jim came away from this session so energized that he still thinks about Tufte's advice when he creates charts in his consulting practice.

During our interview with Boris Esterkes of adidas, he stated that part of being a good designer is being an energizer for those around him. He said that better results are obtained from design reviews and meetings with an engaging presentation and the right content to inspire the audience. "Flair happens when you excite people," he explained, and "even if your product is boring, if your presentation is great you excite people." Some of Esterkes's tips to energize a meeting are: get straight to the point, be the expert on the story or concept being presented, and love the product. Designers should talk about what they believe in regarding their design concept, Esterkes noted. To set the scene, Esterkes has his designers bring examples of products, trims (zippers, drawstrings, tags, etc.), and graphic treatments to pass around during their presentations, so the audience can participate and become excited by seeing, holding, and touching the new product. Esterkes recommends using anecdotes and funny stories to enliven a talk, but always making sure they're relevant to the subject at hand. Finally, he tells his designers to make the audience feel that what they do is important and that they're the experts on the stories behind the design. "Talk about [the] product with assertiveness," he emphasized.

As part of the design team, Jenn attended most of Esterkes's design reviews and those of his colleagues. One such review that stands out took place in a large, formal meeting room that had been rearranged to feel more like a café than a corporate space – the design staff had moved all the long tables to the edges of the room and set up the chairs in clusters in the center facing the projection screen. A couch, soft chairs, coffee table, and side tables were carried up from the design lounge and interspersed with the standard black office chairs to impart a living room vibe. When the developers, project managers, and rest of the team assembled for the talk, they sat with friends, set up notebooks on their laps, and rested drinks and snacks on the side tables. A playlist of current indie hits was playing on a laptop, inviting the participants to relax and disengage their minds from the office tasks they left to attend this meeting. Once the designers finished their presentations, the ideas presented, issues that might arise, and next steps were discussed. Everyone's comments were welcome, as always, which was supported by the communal feeling of the room arrangement and ease of conversation. Jenn remembers this day as very productive yet relaxed and that all team members were involved. She left energized to do her technical drawings of the designs presented, so product samples could be generated, and looked forward to the next meeting with the same team.

Our examples of energizing customers, colleagues, and audiences have something in common – their offerings' flair includes most of the other five SEESEE elements, namely story, entertainment, experience, sincerity, and excellence. Energized customers, colleagues, and audiences, then, arise from offerings that exhibit comprehensive, well-crafted flair. There was already a commitment for the offering to have an energizing capability.

. . .

This chapter completes our presentation on the SEESEE elements of flair. Part III is our "How To" section, where you'll learn how to navigate the four-step process for creating effective flair: (1) define a meaningful and joyful essence for your offering; (2) add flair to achieve the meaningful and joyful essence; (3) validate that the flair is effective; and (4) iterate among these steps.

Essentials: Energy

■ Energy primes people to act.

■ Energy spreads and propels the popularity of an offering.

■ To design flair that energizes, it helps to love the product you're developing.

■ Offerings that energize:

- Contain most of the other five SEESEE attributes: story, entertainment, experience, sincerity, and excellence.

- Show that passion and care went into the design and implementation of the flair.

- Are fun for the designer to create and for the customer to use.

PART III

How to Create Effective Flair

9

Define a Meaningful and Joyful Essence for Your Offering

You can't wait for inspiration; you have to
go after it with a club.
— Jack London, author

W E BEGIN CHAPTER 9 with a quote from Rance Crain's 2014 interview with Sir John Hegarty from *Advertising Age:*

One of the things Sir John learned was that advertising is not science. "We have clients that want advertising to be a science. . . . I think marketing directors go down on their knees every night and plead with God, 'Please can you make it a science?' Sadly, it is not." . . . Selling, Sir John told me, is "an emotional occupation. It's an art. And therefore you have to have your sales messages constructed in such a way that appeals to people. And information goes in through the heart. We are emotional creatures. We are not logical." [1]

Although Sir John's words are about advertising, they apply in the same way to adding flair, which is also about capturing customers' attention and emotions. But while designing flair is a creative endeavor, methodical approaches help. We begin here a four-chapter journey into how to create effective flair using a systematic process:

1. Define a meaningful and joyful essence for your offering (Chapter 9).

2. Add flair to achieve the meaningful and joyful essence (Chapter 10).

3. Validate that the flair is effective (Chapter 11).

4. Iterate among these steps (Chapter 12).

The first step in producing effective flair is defining the meaningful and joyful essence of your offering. Pinpointing this essence provides the basis for determining the flair that will engage both rationally and emotionally and that will be sincere to the offering. By the essence of an offering, we mean the benefit it gives the customer, colleague, or audience, both rationally and emotionally.

The rational view of your offering's benefit can come from asking, in the language of Christensen, what job does your offering do for the user or audience? As mentioned in Chapter 2, a quarter-inch drill will give users what they want, which isn't the quarter-inch drill but a quarter-inch hole. A restaurant patron wants an appetizing and well-presented meal in pleasurable surroundings with hospitable service that come together in an enjoyable dining experience. Colleagues at work want not just factual results from your work but results that show how they will enable the business to thrive.

Besides identifying what an offering does for a customer rationally, understanding the emotional response they'll have to your offering is important. Most offerings have several dimensions that give rise to emotional reactions. In obtaining a quarter-inch hole with a quarter inch drill, there's the gratification of having a good hole (clean, correctly placed, and straight) and the pleasure of having a good experience using the drill (the drill was well-balanced, the grip was comfortable, and the drill bit went through the material as if it were butter). Similarly, a restaurant patron can not only feel delighted with the taste of the food but also impressed with its lovely presentation as well as the restaurant's professional yet friendly service and festive décor. Colleagues will be energized to act on your study results if you've made their use clear, their benefits evident, and their implementation path understandable, and if they feel it's within their and the organization's capabilities to implement your results.

Ask Progressively Deeper "What" Questions to Define the Meaningful and Joyful Essence

One way to define the meaningful and joyful essence is to ask what's at the root of your offering. *Root* is defined by the *Merriam-Webster Unabridged Collegiate Dictionary* as "the essential core."[2] Looking for the root of something can be done by continually drilling down deeper to understand what's at the core. This is what Toyota does when it asks its "five whys" to solve problems in manufacturing.[3] The process is a root cause analysis that involves continually asking, "Why is this failing?" With each answer, Toyota then asks "why" the deeper problem underlying that answer is failing, until no further underlying problem surfaces. Toyota is then at the problem's root cause.

Jim was driving his car along Interstate 95 with the cruise control turned on. When he pressed the brake pedal, the cruise control didn't disengage as it should have. So while he was pressing the brake pedal to stop, the cruise control was trying to maintain the speed. It occurred to him to turn off the cruise control, and then the brakes slowed the car. He had the problem fixed by the dealer, who repaired a broken wire from the switch on the braking mechanism. A year later the same thing happened. This time Jim went to a local independent repair shop. The shop said the same wire had split again and further explained that the wire was too short and was continually being bent when the brake was applied. The repeated flexing caused the wire to weaken until it broke. The shop installed a longer wire with a loop so the wire wouldn't flex and break again.

In analyzing the issue the first time, the dealer asked why the cruise control didn't disengage and then stopped after finding that a wire was broken. The local repair shop, however, asked progressively deeper "why" questions to get to the root cause of the failure. The shop asked why the wire broke and determined that the wire was flexing and weakening. Then they asked why the wire was flexing and found that it was too short, which was the root cause of the cruise control not turning off. This solution fixed the problem permanently, whereas the dealer's failure to look for the underlying cause provided only a temporary fix. The dealer also lost Jim's future patronage.

You can adapt this drill-down process to determine the meaningful and joyful essence of your offering. Instead of asking "why" questions, ask and answer progressively deeper "what" questions, such as "What does this offering do for customers?" Keep asking until you don't get a new answer; at that point, you'll be at the essence. Remember that the answers to the "what" questions should be from the perspective of customers and should reveal emotional and rational aspects about how the customers feel about the offering.

Before asking the deeper "what" questions, there are a few context questions to ask yourself to be sure you understand your offering:

- *Who are the customers for your offering?* – There may be a more than one customer. At work you may be providing study results to your manager, who may in turn extract information for a senior executive. You may be designing a product for children, but parents will make the purchase decision, so you have two customers. So identify all the customers and define their roles in making a decision about your offering.

- *In what situations will your offering be used or experienced?* – Will your offering apply at work, at home, when out and about, or in other situations; in what locations will it apply; will the customer be alone, with others, or both; will the offering need to interact with other things (be connected to power, a car, a bicycle, or other); and will it need to take into account other contexts or situations?

- *What do you want the offering to accomplish?* – What do you want it to do or provide for customers? Will they use it to accomplish a task, have fun, make a decision, or for other purposes? What is the task, what fun, what decision-making?

- *What reaction to your offering would be ideal?* – Do you want your offering purchased, your service enjoyed, your work results used, or others told about your offering? Is the offering expected to change people's behavior and cause them to act? How will it do this?

- *What will be the motivation for people to act on your offering?* – Will they think your offering will do a good job, be pleasant to use or experience, look stylish, or other? Look for an emotional aspect to their motivation.

With an understanding of the context of your offering, begin drilling down with your progressively deeper "what" questions by first asking "What does this offering do for customers?"

- *1st question: What does this offering do for customers?* – It does A.

- *2nd question: What does doing A do?* – It lets someone do B.

- *3rd question: What does doing B do?* – It lets someone do C.

- *4th question: What does doing C do?* – We can't think of a further answer, so we will stop and say the essence of the offering is that is does C.

Now check the essence as you've defined it to see whether it's meaningful and joyful. If it's not, then you need to modify it or go through the process again to come up with a meaningful and joyful essence.

If you're still not sure how to use this drill-down process the following examples demonstrate it applied to specific products, services, and daily work. Please read on – we won't leave you puzzled.

Essence for Products

We'll use the Apple iPod as an example of using drill-down "what" questions to define its meaningful and joyful essence. The essence we defined for the iPod – the joy of music is always with you –

was discussed in chapters one and two. Below is a series of context questions to ask about the iPod to prepare for asking the "what" questions, along with answers that might have been given.

- *Who are the customers for your offering (the iPod)?* – Anyone wanting to listen to an extensive selection of music anywhere they go.

- *In what situations will the offering be used or experienced?* – Anywhere inside or outside, and when doing almost anything.

- *What do you want the offering to accomplish?* – Excite customers with the ability to listen to an extensive selection of music anywhere and anytime.

- *What reaction to your offering would be ideal?* – Customers decide to buy and use.

- *What would be the motivation for people to act on your offering?* – They are excited to listen to an extensive selection of music anywhere and anytime.

Below is a series of "what" questions that might have been asked about the iPod to define its meaningful and joyful essence.

- *1st question: What does the iPod do?* – It's a mobile device that stores and plays music.

- *2nd question: What does a mobile device that stores and plays music do?* – It lets people listen to music wherever they are.

- *3rd question: What does a device that lets people listen to music wherever they are do?* – It lets them always have the joy of music with them.

- *4th question: What does a device that lets someone always have the joy of music with them do?* – We can't think of a further answer, so we'll stop and reword the above answer to say that the essence of the iPod is "the joy of music is always with you."

To get to the essence, we've gone beyond the physical product to what it does for the customer at an emotional level. The essence "the joy of music is always with you" is meaningful since people like to listen to music almost anywhere they are. This was proven by the success of Sony's Walkman and Discman from the 1980s and 1990s. This essence is also joyful since music is exhilarating.

To show how a creative firm designs flair in a product, we turn to our interview with Dominique Fillion of Reebok, with whom Jenn worked for several years. Reebok has an exclusive contract with the National Hockey League to design and supply team uniforms, athlete team training apparel, and fan gear and headwear. During the 2007–2008 NHL season, Reebok introduced an updated pro jersey called the "Reebok Edge." The motivation to revamp the NHL uniform was to give athletes a lighter, more fitted, flexible jersey to improve player performance. Reebok slimmed down the silhouette, added a four-way stretch fabric to create a wider range of mobility, and increased breathability in the mesh. Having less bulk and greater maneuverability conveyed speed and athleticism to the fans and served to enhance player performance. "The big story," Dom explained, "[was] that we had this new uniform that would help player performance" and was "very distinct from a visual standpoint."

Besides providing new uniforms for the pro athletes, Reebok designs and sells fan gear and retail versions of the players' uniforms and training apparel, the design of which will be the focus of our analysis. For the players, the essence of the new NHL Edge jerseys is straightforward: improved player maneuverability with greater stretch, ergonomic fit, and better ventilation. To define the meaningful and joyful essence for fan gear, we'll go through the context questions and then the "what" questions. The Reebok design team may not have addressed the exact questions listed below, but Fillion did discuss the topics raised in these questions.

- *Who are the customers for your offering (new NHL uniforms and fan gear)?* – NHL players and fans.

- *In what situations will the offering be used or experienced?* – The new uniforms will be worn during all NHL games and will be seen by fans when they attend games and watch on television. Fan gear based on the new Edge system will be displayed in stores and online.

- *What do you want the offering to accomplish?* – Excite the fans about the players' new uniforms that enhanced performance and about the new fan gear based on the Edge design.

- *What reaction to your offering would be ideal?* – Fans buy new fan gear for their team based on what they see the players wearing.

- *What would be the motivation for people to act on your offering?* – The new uniforms stand out as innovative, unique, and exciting.

Now we're ready for the series of "what" questions to define the meaningful and joyful essence of Reebok's updated NHL fan gear.

- *1st question: What will the new NHL uniforms do for fans?* – They'll notice the new uniform design on players with a slimmed-down silhouette, better fabric technology, and more prominent logo and graphic placement.

- *2nd question: What will noticing new uniforms on players with a slimmed-down silhouette, better fabric technology, and more prominent logo and graphic placement do for fans?* – Fans will be excited by the sleek appearance and the new technology incorporated in the uniforms.

- *3rd question: What will being excited by the sleeker appearance and the new technology incorporated in the uniforms do for fans?* – Fans will be excited by the updated fan gear based on the new player uniforms.

- *4th question: What will being excited by the updated fan gear based on the new player uniforms do for fans?* – We can't think of a further answer, so we'll stop and say the essence of the fan gear is "the excitement of having updated NHL gear based on the new player uniforms."

This essence implies that Reebok wasn't just making new NHL uniforms for the players but was incorporating updated design elements and technology in the revamped uniforms in a way that fans would notice when watching games. As Fillion noted, "the consumer can visually see and notice the uniform is different than where it has been in the past." The new design elements were used to raise fan excitement in the game and for their teams and to motivate the fans to buy the updated fan gear. The essence covers stories and experiences that the new uniforms convey about hockey and the team – speed and athleticism – and fans, in their new gear, would feel part of their team.

Essence for Services

For an example of defining the meaningful and joyful essence of a service, we turn again to Lyons/Zaremba, the Boston-based exhibit design firm. During our interview, Steve Lenox described designing the *Amazon and Beyond* exhibit at Zoo Miami. This twenty-seven-acre exhibit displays the forests of Central and South America, which include three ecoregions: the Cloud Forest, the Amazon Forest, and the South American Atlantic Forest. Cloud forests cover higher grounds shrouded in moisture and mist. The Amazon rainforest flourishes along the Amazon basin where the rivers swell and overflow their banks every year flooding the forests. The Atlantic Forest contains two separate but similar ecosystems: the Mata Atlântica, which comprises tropical and subtropical forests along the Atlantic coast, and the Pantanal, which is the largest freshwater wetland in the world. In the exhibit, a South American-styled central outdoor plaza connects the three forest regions into one cohesive concept.

Lenox described how Lyons/Zaremba began the *Amazon and Beyond* exhibit design, as it begins all its design efforts, in work sessions with the client to define not what the visitors will see in the exhibit but what is desired to "transform how [the visitors] think and feel about something." Lyons/Zaremba and the client developed stories that visitors of all ages and backgrounds might tell after their experience at *Amazon and Beyond*. "When kids come home from a trip to your facility," Lenox asked, "what stories do you want to hear them say and what stories will they tell their families?"

The *Amazon and Beyond* exhibit displayed three unique regions, so their differences needed to be conveyed along with any distinctive messages and conservation issues. For example, the higher ground areas of cloud forests are quiet and moist, with a mysterious quality. The lush Amazon rainforest contains large animals, such as anaconda snakes, which are 20 feet long and weight 300 pounds on average, and massive vegetation, including cannonball trees that grow to 115 feet. The Atlantic Forest is dryer than the other ecoregions, and much of this area has been lost to human clearing for cultivation, thus environmental issues needed to be conveyed to visitors. Each region needed its own distinct stories and experiences, and the exhibit had to capture the essence of the Amazon region as a whole.

The information gathered in the work sessions with the client – stories visitors will tell and how their thinking will be transformed – provided the basis for developing the content, designing the exhibits, and adding flair. Before delving into the design process, the essence of what the *Amazon and Beyond* exhibit will provide to visitors needed to be defined. While Lyons/Zaremba may not have addressed these exact questions in its design efforts, Lenox readily answered these questions during our interview about the *Amazon and Beyond* design process.

- *Who are the customers for your offering (the* Amazon and Beyond *exhibit)?* – People of all ages and nationalities, especially families, visiting Miami.

- *In what situations will the offering be used or experienced?* – *Amazon and Beyond* is an exhibit area within Zoo Miami that presents three different Amazon ecoregions within an integrated experience. It will likely be visited with family, friends, or school groups. It may be visited as part of a vacation to Miami.

- *What do you want the offering to accomplish?* – Show the varied Amazon ecoregions, explain their current fragility, and inspire visitors to appreciate and think further about these habitats.

- *What reaction to your offering would be ideal?* – Excitement about the diversity, richness, and uniqueness of the Amazon region. Awareness of the fragility of the ecoregions.

- *What would be the motivation for people to act on your offering?* – Visit the *Amazon and Beyond* exhibit because they heard exciting things about it from others, enjoy the visit and tell stories about it to others, and become conscious of how their actions may affect the fragile Amazon region.

Now we can define a meaningful and joyful essence for *Amazon and Beyond* at Zoo Miami by asking the series of "what" questions. Again, Lyons/Zaremba didn't answer these questions with the exact wording below, but our discussion with Lenox uncovered similar reasoning.

- *1st question: What will a visit to* Amazon and Beyond *do for visitors?* – They will experience three Amazon ecoregions.

- *2nd question: What will experiencing the three Amazon ecoregions do for visitors?* – It will let them enjoy the richness and uniqueness of the habitats and become aware of the fragility of that environment.

- *3rd question: What will enjoying the richness and uniqueness of the habitats and becoming aware of the fragility of that environment do for visitors?* – It will let them form experiences and stories about their visit to internalize and share with others; it will increase their knowledge and change their thinking about the Amazon region.

- *4th question: What will forming experiences and stories about their visit to internalize and share with others along with increasing their knowledge and changing their thinking about the Amazon region do for visitors?* – It will provide the joy of discovery to gain experiences, stories, knowledge, and new understanding about the Amazon region.

- *5th question: What will providing the joy of discovery by developing personal experiences, stores, and knowledge about the Amazon region do for visitors?* – We can't think of a further answer, so we'll stop and say the essence of *Amazon and Beyond* is "the joy of discovery to gain experiences, stories, knowledge, and new understanding about the Amazon region."

The essence of joy of discovery implies that *Amazon and Beyond* isn't just an exhibit where people observe plants and animals one by one and read labels that describe what they're looking at. Rather it provides experiences in which visitors can absorb the sights, sounds, feelings, and moods of three Amazon ecoregions. The essence implies that visitors will have stories to tell about their discoveries when they go home, to school, or to work – the visit will feel like an exploratory journey through the region. Finally, the essence suggests that visitors will learn about the fragile state of the Amazon region and will change their thinking about it. In summary, objectives for the exhibit include creating experiences, building stories visitors can share, and elevating their understanding of the Amazon region. These goals provide the basis for designing the flair that will evoke the meaningful and joyful essence that visitors to the exhibit will experience. How Lyons/Zaremba designed flair with Zoo Miami so *Amazon and Beyond* delivered this meaningful and joyful essence is explained in Chapter 10.

Essence for Daily Work

Jim identified benefits and performance measures for an FAA air traffic control improvement program known as Safe Flight 21, which was aimed at increasing safety and efficiency of flight operations. While employed at the Volpe Center, Jim participated with the program's Cost-Benefit Subgroup, formed in the summer of 1999. He facilitated workshops with representatives from the FAA, United Airlines, UPS, and the Aircraft Owners and Pilots Association (an organization of owners and pilots of small private airplanes) where benefits were identified and defined for each of the twenty-one projects in the FAA program. Performance measures for the benefits were also developed.

To focus the workshops on providing information about benefits and measures for each project, Jim and a co-worker, Jack Perkins, defined the essence of the effort. Context questions about the measures were:

- *Who are the customers for your offering (benefit definitions and performance measures for Safe Flight 21)?* – FAA managers, airline and cargo carriers, and small private aircraft pilots and owners.

- *In what situations will the offering be used or experienced?* – For review, comment, and decision-making by the participants as to how the Safe Flight 21 projects affect them.

- *What do you want the offering to accomplish?* – Subgroup members and other managers can easily use the benefit definitions and performance measures to help make decisions.

- *What reaction to your offering would be ideal?* – Appreciation for the clarity and usefulness of the benefit definitions and performance measures.

- *What would be the motivation for people to act on your offering?* – The feeling that they have sufficient, meaningful, and clear information to study to help them make decisions regarding the Safe Flight 21 program.

The drill-down questions asked to get to the meaningful and joyful essence of the benefit definitions and performance measures are:

- *1st question: What will the benefit definitions and performance measures do?* – They will provide information about the projects.

- *2nd question: What will information about the projects do?* – It will provide an understanding of the benefits contributed by each project.

- *3rd question: What will providing an understanding of the benefits contributed by each project do?* – It will help the participants make decisions about the program.

- *4th question: What will helping the participants make decisions about the program do?* – We can't think of a further answer, so we'll stop and say the essence of the benefit definitions and performance measures is "to help the participants make decisions about the program."

The meaningful and joyful essence "to help the participants make decisions about the program" may seem simplistic, but recall the NASA example from Chapter 1 – in developing air traffic control performance measures the consulting firm didn't consider the decisions that needed to be made or the information desired by decision-makers. NASA found the performance measures unusable. The essence of the Safe Flight 21 program implies that meaningful and joyful performance measures will address the needs and decision styles of all participants. Chapter 10 will explain how the Safe Flight 21 benefits were defined and the performance measures developed to be meaningful for decision-making by the FAA and industry participants and joyful by providing an easily understood story of how each project's capabilities provide benefits.

Evolving an Essence

A company may have an offering for which it has already defined a meaningful and joyful essence, and later it decides to add other capabilities. The essence, then, will need to be revised to include the changes. StumbleUpon provides an example of doing just this. To learn about the evolution of StumbleUpon we talked with CEO Mark Bartels in October 2014. StumbleUpon, available on desktop and mobile devices, is an Internet discovery engine. Internet search engines, such as Google, Bing, and Yahoo Search, strive to provide the one best response to a user query. StumbleUpon, in contrast, searches for a range of content about the topic of interest in order to supply information the user has likely not seen before. Users can easily click through results to discover web pages, photos, videos, and music personalized to their interests.

In using StumbleUpon Jim selected the categories of blues music, books, computer graphics, folk music, gardening, and humor as his frequently accessed topics. Next he chose blues as a topic to explore, and related websites were displayed. He was able to view the suggestions or click for another recommendation. If he liked the content he could click a thumbs-up button, and if he didn't he could click a thumbs-down button. In this manner StumbleUpon learned his interests for future recommendations. During a query on StumbleUpon about blues music, the site displayed several boogie-woogie pianists, which excited Jim since he likes boogie-woogie and rarely comes across it.

The essence of StumbleUpon's original capability, the discovery of new information, might be stated as "the excitement of discovery." The discovery of information isn't new – for years people have used magazines, newspapers, television channel surfing, and store browsing to find new information – but StumbleUpon now satisfies this desire for discovery on the Internet.

Besides simply making discoveries, users want meaningful and intriguing discoveries, which can come from, as Bartels says, curation and discovery. People have long been taking advantage of curation to make quality discoveries in other media, such as trusting the operator of a second-hand book store to select desirable books or relying on like-minded friends or acquaintances for recommendations. StumbleUpon ensures quality, personalization, and trust for its suggestions through curation involving both algorithms and human experts. The algorithms use criteria such as whether the users click on the thumbs-up or thumbs-down button when they view a discovered site, as well as discovery results that others with similar tastes have liked. For the human aspect of curation, certain users are designated as experts based on having likes and dislikes similar to other users. Content is routinely pushed to these experts to see if they like it. If they do then it's considered quality content to be provided to general users.

StumbleUpon is currently evolving to enable users to share and chat about their discoveries with friends, acquaintances, and online communities with similar interests. Here are context questions and answers that might have been asked to prepare for asking the "what" questions about extending StumbleUpon to encompass sharing and chatting. StumbleUpon did not follow our precise process, but its design effort for the sharing and chatting capability reflects the spirit of our approach.

- *Who are the customers for your offering (extending StumbleUpon to encompass sharing and chatting)?* – Existing and new users of StumbleUpon.

- *In what situations will the offering be used or experienced?* – When using StumbleUpon on a computer or mobile device, when users desire to share and chat about their discoveries, and when users receive discoveries shared by others.

- *What do you want the offering to accomplish?* – Excite fans to use StumbleUpon more often and stay longer. Attract new users.

- *What reaction to your offering would be ideal?* – Be excited by the new sharing and chatting capabilities.

- *What would be the motivation for people to act on your offering?* – Users desire to share and chat about discoveries.

Following our methodology of asking progressively deeper "what" questions to get to the meaningful and joyful essence, sample questions to define the essence of the chatting and sharing capabilities in StumbleUpon might be:

- *1st question: What will the capability for users to share and chat about their discoveries do?* – It will let users share their excitement about discoveries and learn more about the discovery topic from friends and community.

- *2nd question: What will letting users share their excitement about discoveries and learn more about the discovery topic from friends and community do?* – It will combine the excitement of discovery and the joy of sharing the discovery.

- *3rd question: What will combining the excitement of discovery and the joy of sharing do?* – We cannot think of a further answer, so we'll stop and say the extended essence of StumbleUpon is "the excitement of discovery and the joy of sharing."

Certainly this essence is meaningful and joyful to Stumble-Upon's users.

Essentials: Define a Meaningful and Joyful Essence for Your Offering

▨ A four-step structured approach will help you create effective flair:

1. Define a meaningful and joyful essence for your offering.

2. Add flair to achieve the meaningful and joyful essence.

3. Validate that the flair is effective.

4 Iterate among these steps.

▨ The essence of an offering is the benefit it gives the customer, expressed both rationally and emotionally.

● For the rational view, ask what job the offering does for the customer.

● For the emotional view, ask what emotional response a customer will have to your offering.

▨ Ask context questions to be sure you fully understand your offering.

▨ Determine a meaningful and joyful essence of your offering by asking and answering progressively deeper "what" questions, as in "What does this do for the users or audience?"

▨ Check if the essence is meaningful and joyful. If not, modify it, or define a new essence.

10

Add Flair to Achieve the Meaningful and Joyful Essence

Inspiration is for amateurs.

— Chuck Close, painter and photographer

DEFINING THE MEANINGFUL AND JOYFUL ESSENCE of an offering is the starting point for building effective flair – what the flair should enhance and how to keep the flair sincere. Too often companies and individuals start adding flair before they understand the essence, which can lead to ineffective, even silly, flair. This chapter continues the how-to-add-effective-flair progression from defining the meaningful and joyful essence of an offering that we discussed in Chapter 9 to how to design and add flair once the offering's essence is defined.

There are no precise steps to take in designing flair, since it isn't a precise concept. Most companies and individuals who are successful at design that energizes, however, use structured approaches to build flair. We've assembled a structured approach derived from our interviews with designers, research on companies that are successful with design, and observations of instances of good flair. Our interviewees include a professional dance company director, two design directors at sports fashion companies, the president of a firm that designs exhibition space, a fine arts museum curatorial manager, and the CEO of a firm that designs web and mobile user experience interfaces. We've also looked at inspirational companies such as Apple, Target, Zappos, and Beats, and we've examined best practices in such fields as fashion design, graphic design, and narrative journalism.

To illustrate that artists and designers do use processes and that these processes can be adapted for building flair into your offering, we present the creation of an original dance performance. Reviewing a creative process from start to finish will, we hope, drive home the point that designing flair isn't something done only by those with an artistic bent who readily find inspiration, but that anyone can design flair by following a structured process.

Using a Structured Approach to Create a Dance Performance

Deborah Abel is a modern dancer and choreographer who is Artistic Director of the Deborah Abel Dance Company and runs a school of modern dance in the Boston area. We talked with Abel about her choreography process and what makes a dance performance a success. Like the creative professionals we interviewed at Reebok, adidas, Lyon/Zaremba, Fresh Tilled Soil, and other firms, Abel uses a structured process in her creations. She begins by defining a concept, or essence, of a new dance and then follows a systematic approach to develop a cohesive narrative and to add meaningful and joyful flair.

In 2012 Abel's dance company premiered her original work entitled "Calling to You: A Tale of Ancient Wisdom in the Modern

World." When they're beginning to develop a new dance, Abel and her husband, Lee Perlman, who is the music director of the company, decide what they want to say through the performance. For this dance they decided to tell an ancient love story from India and update it to relate to a modern couple. With this general concept they began researching classic Indian tales from such sources as the *Mahabharata* and the *Bhagavad Gita* to find an Indian love story on which to build their dance narrative.

For "Calling to You" they ultimately selected a parable from a book called *Yoga and the Quest for the True Self* by Stephen Cope. In this parable the son of a king is kidnapped as a child and grows into adulthood far from his home. As he matures the child experiences a journey of self-discovery and eventually finds his way back to the kingdom as a confident man ready to take over rule from his father. Abel thought the narrative of the journey and personal growth was wonderful, but it was missing the story of love that they wanted to incorporate into the dance. So Abel and Perlman kept the parable's essence of self-discovery but adapted it to tell the story of a boy and girl, in love as children, who through calamity are separated from each other and from their village, grow through their own personal journeys, and are reunited as adults to fully realize their love.

Abel and Perlman constructed the performance as seven dance sequences covering stages of the children's separate personal growth, reconnection as fully realized adults, and rekindled love. The first dance introduces a contemporary couple who can no longer connect or understand why they're so troubled. The dance then turns to the ancient couple as children in love, living in the same village only to be torn apart by a calamity that causes them to separately leave the village and eventually forget one another.

The second dance portrays the boy's time spent with the Sadhus, holy men who live in the mountains away from society to seek their spirituality. Abel describes this dance as study and meditation with the Sadhus that focuses inward on personal growth. The third dance portrays the girl at the Temple of the Mother, where she lives with the priestesses and learns about the feminine view of love, care, and healing of all beings. In the fourth dance the young man enters a perilous forest and is attacked by tiger spirits – a vibrant and exciting dance (see Exhibit 10.1).

In the fifth dance, the priestesses find the injured man and bring him to their Temple of the Mother to be healed. At first the young man and woman don't recognize one another, but as he recovers they remember each other and dance to celebrate their renewed love. Since they each grew to complete adults on their own, they're now able to come together as whole, mature individuals to find true love. The sixth dance is a quartet with the young man and woman from the ancient story showing the contemporary couple how to reconnect and love one another. Finally, the performance concludes with a joyous dance of the contemporary couple celebrating their togetherness and full realization of being soul mates.

The above summary of the robust choreography inspired by this narrative journey simplifies the rigorous and complex two-year process to craft the performance. For the choreography, Abel created and collected movements and dance phrases. Many dance moves were developed during her adult classes and fleshed out for later use. All rehearsals were videotaped and studied. When we asked Abel to delineate her creative process in precise steps, she laid out the following phases:

1. Define the concept.

2. Develop and collect dance movements.

Exhibit 10.1. Scene from the Tiger Spirit piece of "Calling to You: A Tale of Ancient Wisdom in the Modern World" with dancers Alonso Guzman, Joe Gonzalez, and Tony Tucker of the Deborah Abel Dance Company. Photo by Liza Voll. Note how Abel captures the vibrant and energetic spirit of this dance portion through her choreography, scenery, and choice of dancers.

3. Compose music.

4. Begin dance rehearsals.

5. Rehash rehearsals, story details, and music composition. Iterate among these elements so that all aspects work together to tell the story.

Perlman composed an original musical score for this narrative. Some of the music was completed before rehearsals, but as the choreography evolved and lengthened the music was modified and expanded to fit the evolving dance.

To validate that the dance performance being created was still central to the concept, Abel and Perlman analyzed the video of every rehearsal for storyline as well as artistry. Abel said: "I think it's an inner experience. Is it ringing true or is it straying? . . . We are trying to create an experience. We are aiming straight for the heart. We are bypassing the mind." Abel continued, "Essence, essence, essence. That's the way they are going to remember this experience." When we asked Abel to define the essence of "Calling to You," she quickly responded that it is to create an experience for the audience centering on love and re-finding love, and that the more people are fully realized as themselves, the healthier and stronger their relationships will be.

The flair elements of SEESEE can be seen in Abel and Perlman's dynamic dance concert. We've already explored the *story* in the performance expressing universal relationship struggles and the rewards of re-finding love. Conveying this message straight to the heart through dance movement and original music creates an emotional, dynamic *experience* for the viewer. Abel's dance, of course, *entertains*. As previously noted, Abel and Perlman made sure the evolution of the piece related to the story and essence through all iterations of crafting – this made the dance *sincere*. *Excellence* shows through the careful choices of choreography, music, dancers, and costumes as well as rigorous rehearsals. Finally, all the love and dedication Abel and Perlman put into this dance concert are sure to leap off the stage and *energize* the audience.

Artists and designers use structured processes to create their works. Designing flair is not about waiting for inspiration but following a process.

An Approach to Designing Flair

We delineate four general steps to take in designing flair. We encourage you to try the techniques, adopt what works for you, modify the steps to better suit your needs, and add steps that you think will help in your work.

Step 1: Conduct research and gather observations on ideas for flair.

Before generating ideas for flair, conducting background research on past and current uses of flair within and outside your firm is so helpful that we consider it essential. Consider what was successful and unsuccessful in your company's experiences; in offerings by others in your industry; and in products, services, and daily work that are outside your industry but that may have a similar message. We recommend that you conduct research and gather observations both as ongoing activities and as exercises aimed at a particular flair design effort. Gathering and recording flair design ideas that you observe and that occur to you independent of any particular flair effort will provide a rich source of ready ideas when it comes time to add flair to a specific offering. For your daily work, note what others do particularly well or reports that you thought were intriguing and clear.

At the beginning of Part I we quoted a professor at Cal Arts, who said that design is all around us. So look around and note appealing flair that you might adapt for your use. Jenn does what many designers do and keeps journals where she jots notes or draws pictures of designs she observes and ideas she creates. Jim keeps lists of ideas on his computer under different file headings, and scans and stores clippings of articles with promising design ideas. Just the process of recording these inspirational observations will expand your scope of creative ideas and understanding of how design can evoke an emotional response.

Step 2: Identify touch points for adding flair.

Flair might be in the physical appearance of a product, such as shape, size, color, and texture; in the operation of a product, such as navigating a smartphone, operating a kitchen appliance, or pushing buttons on an automobile dashboard; in the interaction with a service, such as waitstaff, sales staff, or phone customer service representatives; in the décor of a restaurant or store; or in the format of a business presentation or report.

To identify and understand the touch points of an offering, look for ways in which the customer interacts with the offering, and characterize how the engagement at that touch point will occur. For a product, this might be seeing the object, picking it up, operating it, and obtaining something from using it. For a service, this might be a customer entering and being in a store, restaurant, or place featuring the service; interacting with the staff; and participating in the service. For daily work, this might include your audience listening to a presentation or reading a report of your work, understanding the content of your work, and understanding what could be done with your results.

Step 3: Identify what constitutes a good experience from the touch points.

Examine the touch points identified in Step 2 to determine what constitutes a stimulating experience for the customer interacting with each touch point. Possible customer experiences with the touch points for a *product* are: (1) for viewing the product – being attracted to a stylish shape, color, and texture; (2) for holding the product – being pleased with its size, texture, and shape; (3) for operating the product – being gratified by its quick, easy, and obvious functioning; and (4) for using the product – considering its result effective and enjoyable. For *service* touch points, possible customer experiences are: (1) for being in the place where a service is provided – feeling comfortable in the physical layout and décor; (2) for interacting with the service staff – being delighted with efficiency, tone, and service by the staff; and (3) for participating in the service – feeling pleasure from the experience and thinking fondly of the service after leaving. For *daily work* touch points with colleagues, managers, and audiences, possible experiences are: (1) for listening to a presentation or reading a report of your work – being engaged, intrigued, and excited by the results; (2) for understanding the work's content – feeling that the results are clear and memorable; and (3) for understanding what's to be done with your results – feeling confident that the results can be easily implemented, being excited to follow up to gain more information, being inspired to recommend your results within the organization, or feeling informed enough to make a decision.

Step 4: Develop flair.

Step 2 has shown us where to add flair, and Step 3 has defined what the flair should do to excite at each touch point. Now the design of the flair for the touch points can begin. Flair may not be appropriate or you may not have resources to implement for all the touch points, so select where flair will be most effective. At the same time, you don't want any touch points to produce a negative experience.

The SEESEE elements of flair can serve as starting points to design specific instances of flair. Applying these typically involves brainstorming to think of a story, entertainment, and an experience related to the offering that will be sincere, excellent, and will energize the customer. Consider the aspects of the offering where excellence will be particularly appreciated or where a lack of excellence may be particularly irritating. Examine the likelihood that the flair will energize action. SEESEE can be applied to the overall offering or to specific touch points in the offering. All, some, or one SEESEE element can be used for any one touch point. The development of specific forms of flair also draws upon the ideas generated in the research and observation-gathering activities described in Step 1.

In the remainder of this chapter we'll discuss how companies that we interviewed developed specific instances of flair. There are differences among the techniques used by each company, but all have similar elements within their structured processes to create designs that engage.

Adding Flair to Products

We continue the discussion of the process followed by the designers of the Reebok Sports Licensed Division to create new NHL fan gear. In Chapter 9 we defined the meaningful and joyful essence of Reebok's hockey fan gear as "the excitement of having updated NHL gear based on the new player uniforms." This essence reflects how the new Edge jersey's design elements, which improved pro player performance, can energize fans about the game and the Reebok brand and motivate them to buy new fan gear. How Reebok added flair to achieve the meaningful and joyful essence is explained below. This discussion is drawn from our interview with Dominique Fillion, introduced in Chapter 9.

In one crucial step in the design process, the Reebok team began by examining the new professional players' jerseys from the fans' viewpoint to determine where new detailing would stand out during a game viewed in the stadium or on television. The Reebok team concluded, Fillion explained, that the top of the uniforms is most visible on television, particularly when the camera shows players on the bench. Using the idea of the upper portion of the jersey as the most marketable area, designers envisioned a unique neckline shape that created an iconic look for the NHL and a brand statement for Reebok. The NHL shield logo was then moved to the neck to emphasize brand visualization, as had been done successfully for the NFL. Besides the neckline, the shoulder yoke and seam lines were modified to highlight the redesign of this highly visible "hero zone," as Fillion refers to it, at the top of the jersey.

During the evolution of the Edge system, a color pop of neon green was incorporated into the trim (neck tape, zipper pull, tags) and graphics to enhance awareness of Reebok's advanced technology. This particular green color had already been "happening inside [our] backyard," Fillion said. "As a brand, Reebok hockey [had] been using this green to call out new technology of their product [and] showcase innovation." Reebok skates show the green on a pump that improves fit, and on Reebok's hockey O-sticks the green indicates the composite material that increases power transfer to the puck. The bright green was also team neutral – no NHL teams' color identities incorporated this green.

The neon green NHL performance color pop was placed in the highly visible "hero zone" on the players' uniforms. Neck tape on all pro jerseys and training apparel is neon green. A special plastic grip zipper pull was designed with the green knit into the zipper cords for the center front and pocket zippers on the players' team apparel. Fans readily see this green color pop.

The bright green was also incorporated into fan replica jerseys and retail apparel so fans could identify with the performance gear worn by the pro athletes. On the fan apparel, the green is used in the neck tape and zipper pulls, as well as in special detailing, such as stitching around an earbud access slit in a pocket. The green was also added to price tags, posters, and retail advertising to brand as Reebok products. In stores, the green pop identified Reebok as the official retailer of the NHL and made the fan gear easy to locate among the sea of products.

The bright green color came from a logical source – Reebok's innovative hockey equipment – and already had a meaningful and joyful essence of highlighting the new performance technology in the equipment. And the color pop was easily transferable to pro and retail apparel. But identifying meaningful and joyful design ideas such as this involves a lengthy research, brainstorming, and creation process. Fillion described a process that begins with understanding a need to fill in the market and then identifying how and why Reebok can fulfill that need. At the beginning of a new design effort, designers travel locally, nationally, and internationally to observe the market in all design arenas (concerts, fashion hot spots such as New York City, automobiles, trendy shopping areas such as Los Angeles) and question users about their needs and wants in sports fashion products. Brainstorm sessions are conducted with Reebok design team members as well as with marketing, product managers, development, and technical design to consider all aspects of the product. While careful planning and research are necessary for successful design, Fillion emphasized, a good designer's gut instinct also plays a role. Designers can narrow down their options by looking at something and feeling "that resonates with me," Fillion stated.

Reebok built on past successes – the neon green accent in hockey equipment – and observations of fashion elsewhere – the hole for earbud access to the music device pocket. Reebok looked for touch points where the fans would notice the characteristics of the new pro uniforms, and they considered what would create excitement for fans around these touch points.

Elements of SEESEE are seen in Reebok's design effort. The green trim was part of a story that indicated new technology in Reebok gear and that unified hockey equipment, uniforms, and retail apparel into the Reebok hockey brand. Fans were *entertained* by the speed and athleticism conveyed by the new uniforms. An *experience* was created for fans who saw the new jerseys at hockey games and then saw the new design elements reflected in fan gear for them to purchase. The flair of the green trim was *sincere* since it related to the Reebok tradition of innovation and technology in hockey. Reebok has high standards and an established process in design, development, and delivery, so equipment and clothing provided *excellence*. Finally, fans were *energized* by the new, innovative Edge uniforms and thus by Reebok as a hockey brand.

In the next chapter we'll discuss how the Reebok hockey gear flair was validated before launch.

Adding Flair to Services

As discussed in the previous chapter, Lyons/Zaremba's design of the *Amazon and Beyond* exhibit at Zoo Miami represents three ecoregions of Central and South America. Through asking a series of "what" questions, the essence of the *Amazon and Beyond* exhibit was defined as "the joy of discovery to gain experiences, stories, knowledge, and new understanding about the Amazon region."

Lyons/Zaremba captured this essence by incorporating flair into the *Amazon and Beyond* design that engages all the senses and sets an appropriate mood in each region. The characteristics of each ecoregion are reflected through music, graphics, plant life, animals, sounds, and smells so that the visitor is immersed rationally, emotionally, and sensorially into each habitat. The three ecoregions are linked by a central plaza that conveys their connectedness, and the Lyons/Zaremba team designed the visuals, music, and layouts to achieve cohesion throughout the exhibit. The components of the three exhibit spaces, however, are also tailored to create a unique experience in each area.

The passage of a visitor through each ecoregion exhibit was traced by Lyons/Zaremba to identify how the experience could be enhanced through music, display structure, pathways through the exhibit, and educational signage – identifying and examining touch points. Music for each exhibit was composed by Wall Street Productions and directed by Paul Erikson, a musician and content consultant for Lyons/Zaremba. In our discussion about defining each exhibit, Lenox described the Cloud Forest as being all about quiet. Since cloud forests are at higher elevations shrouded in clouds and moisture, soft music was created, inspired by animal noises but also somewhat mysterious to reflect the misty surroundings. Lulling sound effects contributed to the mystical vibe, and the signage and placards used subtle colors. In the Amazon rainforest the cyclical flooding of the massive river basin produces an ecoregion that's grand, shining, and robust. Thus the music composed for the Amazon Forest is bold and energetic, and the scenery is colorful, large, and loud. Visitors hear animal howls, smell the scent of succulent flowers, and are guided by vibrant graphics. The Atlantic Forest is drier than the other ecoregions, and more than 85 percent of the forest has been lost because of human repurposing such as clearing for crops and grazing.[1] The exhibit was designed to reflect this drier, fragile landscape that has a perilous future. Evidence of erosion and decay was built into the displays so that visitors can realize the perilous future of this region. The music has a melancholy tone. Another non-visual experience in each exhibit space is the sound of insects, wind, and leaves rustling. The smells of blossoms were integrated into the scenes, including flowers that might not always be in bloom so that visitors can have a complete experience of the ecoregions' flowers.

Lyons/Zaremba's design process is collaborative, with brainstorms and discussions that include designers, clients, engineers, construction firms, and maintenance staff. Lyons/Zaremba strives for all participants to be comfortable and takes the attitude that its firm is just part of the team. Input is solicited from all disciplines to gain varying points of view, but Lyons/Zaremba provides design direction and directs the overall concept development.

Lyons/Zaremba identified touch points where visitors could interact with the exhibits through sight, sound, smell, and touch as well as make discoveries that would inspire their understanding. Desired experiences at these touch points were defined.

The elements of SEESEE are reflected in *Amazon and Beyond*. The exhibit was designed for visitors to create *stories* of their discoveries to take away and share. Exotic animals, beautiful plant life, and forest sounds both *entertain* and create special *experiences*. Remaining *sincere* to the region, the added flair mirrors the aura of each ecoregion, and the flair is done with *excellence*, such as the music being specially composed for each exhibit. Finally, visitors are *energized* to appreciate and think further about how their actions can affect the environment.

Adding Flair to Daily Work

In Chapter 9 we covered how Jim and co-worker Jack Perkins defined the essence of benefit definitions and performance measures for the FAA Safe Flight 21 program. The essence was to help the participants make decisions about the program.

We'll now cover making the benefit definitions and performance measures meaningful and joyful for the Safe Flight 21 team. Meaningful means that the definitions and measures would help the Safe Flight 21 participants make a success of the development program, and joyful means that the definitions and measures would be easy to use and would tell the story of the program's benefits. Jim facilitated workshops with the program's Cost-Benefit Subgroup, which comprised representatives from the FAA, United Airlines, UPS, and the Aircraft Owners and Pilots Association.

Jim and Perkins used the four general steps described earlier in this chapter to design flair. For Step 1 (conduct research and collect observations on ideas for flair) Jim continually reviewed documents and presentations on aviation performance measures produced by FAA, NASA, aircraft manufacturers, airlines, cargo carriers, and universities. Step 2 (identify touch points for adding flair) consisted of determining how the Safe Flight participants would likely use the benefit definitions and performance measures and for what purposes. To identify this Jim guided the workshop discussions so that all participants expressed the desires of their organizations regarding reviewing and making decisions about the

Safe Flight 21 benefits. Moving on to Step 3 (identify what constitutes a good experience for the touch points), Jim again worked with the subgroup to characterize the types of decisions to be made, define what information about the benefits and measures would enable all participants to make better decisions, and what presentation form would be best to disseminate information for easy decision-making.

When beginning Step 4 (develop flair), Jim realized that some team members were concentrating only on how the new technology would affect their individual flight operations and not thinking beyond to overall benefits, such as total time and fuel savings. To address this, Jim needed to figure out how to present benefit definitions in a way that the team members could relate the technology to what they would gain. The approach he chose was to tell the story of how the new technology capabilities would be used by the FAA and aircraft operators to obtain the benefits. The narrative elements were the capabilities provided by the new technology, how they were used by pilots and air traffic controllers, and how the pilots' and controllers' actions would create benefits. Performance measures were developed for the direct impacts of pilots and controllers using each capability and for the end user benefits. The story is expressed by showing the flow of the narrative elements in creating the defined benefits. The project capabilities lead to direct impacts, which are measured to clearly demonstrate the level of those impacts. These direct impacts result in end user benefits, which are measured to clearly demonstrate the level of those benefits. Figure 10.2 tells the benefit story of one sample Safe Flight 21 project, Enhanced Visual Approaches.

Several elements of SEESEE were used in designing flair for this offering. Jim drew upon *story* to explain how each project's

Project Capabilities	Direct Impacts	Direct Impact Measures	End User Benefits	End User Benefit Measures
Display in cockpit of nearby aircraft	Pilot able to better identify the aircraft to follow

Pilot awareness of all proximate aircraft positions | Pilot response time to locate other aircraft being indicated by controller

Flight time during arrival to touchdown

Fuel burned during arrival | Reduced arrival delays

Increased predictability of arrival times

Increased airport capacity | **Safety:**

Accident rate during final approach maneuvers

Rate of pilot deviations in terminal area

Efficiency:

Arrival rate

Flight time to fly arrival flight path

FAA Cost Savings:

Voice channel occupancy time savings |

Exhibit 10.2. Performance measures flow chart for the Safe Flight 21 Enhanced Visual Approaches Project.

technology capabilities would provide benefits. *Experience* was considered by making the benefit definitions and performance measures fit the way all the participants made decisions. The flair was *sincere* since the definitions and measures related to the participants' needs and reflected the individual projects, and it showed *excellence* since they were valid and useful.

Reebok, Lyons/Zaremba, and Jim added flair to make the essence of their projects meaningful and joyful. In each of these cases, aspects of the general structured approach to designing flair described in this chapter were used. We hope it's clear that this approach can be used to add flair to almost any product, service, or daily work, and that the flair will reflect the offering's meaningful and joyful essence.

> # Essentials: Add Flair to Achieve the Meaningful and Joyful Essence
>
> - The meaningful and joyful essence of your offering is the starting point for building effective flair.
>   - It provides the definition of what the flair should enhance.
>   - It guides you in terms of how to keep the flair sincere.
> - There are no precise steps to take in designing flair, but there are structured approaches.
> - One approach to designing flair has four steps:
>   1 Conduct research and gather observations on ideas for flair.
>   2 Identify touch points for adding flair.
>   3 Identify what constitutes a good experience from the touch points.
>   4 Develop flair.
> - The six SEESEE elements of flair can serve as starting points to design specific instances of flair.

- Brainstorm to think of a story, entertainment, and/ or experience related to the offering that will be sincere, excellent, and that will energize.

- Consider where excellence will be appreciated or where a lack of excellence may be irritating.

- Draw upon ideas generated in the research and observation-gathering activities.

- Examine the likelihood that the flair will energize action.

11

Validate That the Flair
Is Effective

*Doubt the conventional wisdom unless you can verify
it with reason and experiment.*

— Steve Albini, musician

THIS CHAPTER DESCRIBES VALIDATING FLAIR to assure that
it makes your offering meaningful and joyful, that it can
be added practically and cost-effectively, and that it doesn't
backfire with negative publicity. Sometimes flair turns out to be ineffective or even creates a negative reaction by customers, as some
examples in this chapter will show. We'll discuss three types of validation of flair:

1. Is the flair effective (that is, does it make your offering
   meaningful and joyful)?

2. Can the flair be added practically?

3. What negative reactions might the flair prompt?

General Practices to Validate Flair

General practices that apply to all three types of validation involve examining the flair from the perspective of your customers. Some questions to ask are: What response does the flair evoke? Is this a desired response? Can the flair be incorporated into the offering; can it be manufactured or produced? How might the flair be misinterpreted?

Groups brainstorming to identify flair elements can examine their ideas from the perspective of all potential customers, taking into account different ages, genders, ethnic backgrounds, and geographic locations. Others in the company, or outside the company, can be asked for their reaction to the flair. Examining the flair ideas in a mockup of their actual form is useful since just visualizing something in your mind makes it easy to overlook production and other issues.

Gathering customer preferences can be effective in validating flair. Any such effort, however, needs to be designed, conducted, and analyzed appropriately to gather substantive information. Robert A. Lutz, in his book *Guts: The Seven Laws of Business that Made Chrysler the World's Hottest Car Company,* which is about his years in the auto industry, talks negatively about using input from customer surveys and focus groups.[1] He thinks that customers don't know what they want, that they want to appear rational so they answer with a practical bent rather than about what really excites them, and that they can't see the future so they give answers based on products that already exist. However, a careful design for gathering customer preferences can mitigate most of these factors. Wording of questions, probing to understand answers, analysis of results (such as looking at the spread or clustering of preferences), observing customer behavior, and handing out samples are some ways to improve the effectiveness of gathering customer preferences.

Is the Flair Meaningful and Joyful?

The question being addressed here is: Will the flair influence customers to buy or use your offering? Effective flair is in the mind of the customer, colleague, audience – whoever will buy or use the offering. So you can judge meaningfulness and joyfulness by placing yourself in their place. For the iPod, the essence we defined was "the joy of music is always with you." That people desire to have music with them was previously proven with the success of Sony's Walkman and Discman. Apple designed the iPod to enhance the meaningful and joyful essence of listening to music by dramatically increasing the number of songs that could be stored, making the device small, making the operation easy, and making the design stylish.

To validate the effectiveness of its new apparel designs, Reebok builds prototypes; gathers feedback from colleagues, friends, and family; and obtains expert comments as the garment moves through the many stages from design through production. Team members constantly check that the product reflects the desired essence through all its iterations and revisions. Even before creation begins, Reebok researches to determine what needs in their market new garments can fill. Reebok examines competitors, searches for successful trends in market niches, and studies opportunities to grow in the athletic market. Knowing the customer allows designers to meet their expectations and tell a story they'll understand. Any new Reebok product needs to connect to what the brand is already doing and act as an extension of the brand. To be a pioneer in the athletic design world, a product must excite customers while remaining true to the brand's identity or essence.

Lyons/Zaremba continually reviews the effectiveness of design elements throughout its design process. The company asks what stories a visitor will take from each aspect of the exhibit design as it's being created. During on-going meetings, clients are asked if a design element is providing the experience they desire. The design elements and integration of the overall exhibit are reviewed from the perspectives of visitors from different age groups, different regions in the United States, and different countries. A sample question is: What might kids do, touch, or see when they get to this part of the exhibit, and what would they experience and learn here? "Tell me," Lenox said he might ask, "what this four-year-old kid is going to get to do." The work succeeds when the design team pays attention to the perspective of each visitor, considers the logistics of the space, and satisfies the goals of the client.

Ideas for adding flair in daily work can be tested with colleagues, presented to clients or management to gain feedback, or even be tested in talks with audiences. During Jim's work with the Safe Flight 21 Cost-Benefit Subgroup, he facilitated workshops and used them to validate that the participants' information needs were being met. When validating client needs he often asks them, "How would you use these measures or these results if you had them?" Then he walks the clients through sample situations to learn how they might use the results and to verify that the results provide what's needed. Jim probes the answers from clients to be sure they're fully thought out. These walk-through exercises provide more valuable insights than just asking clients what they need, since they often don't know in detail what they need.

Conducting trials, whether within or outside the company, is a way to validate flair and tweak it to get it right. Before opening the first Apple Store, Steve Jobs built a mock-up of the store in a warehouse near Apple headquarters in Cupertino. In his *Steve Jobs* book, Walter Isaacson describes how the store mock-up was kept secret from the Apple board, which was skeptical of selling through Apple Stores.[2] The physical design, store worker experience, and customer experience were modeled, critiqued, and reworked. Prototypes were built of the entrance, product displays, and handheld checkout system (instead of a cash register counter). Building and tweaking the store mock-up continued for more than six months. Jobs made solo visits and convened a brainstorming session in the store every Tuesday. Upon visiting the store, Apple board member and Gap CEO Millard "Mickey" Drexler, who had suggested building the prototype store, commented that the space was too chopped up and had too many distracting architectural features and colors. So the store was revised. Ron Johnson, who was then in charge of Apple Stores, remarked to Jobs when the store design was almost complete that the store should be organized around what customers might want to do with Apple products rather than around the Apple products themselves. After initially opposing the idea, Jobs changed his mind and the store was revised over several more months. Thus the prototype store was critical in developing the Apple Store concept, visualizing the implementation, and revamping it to get it right.

Simpler and less costly prototype experiences can also provide useful information about flair in a product or service before it's launched. For example, Reebok creates digital 3D renderings to mock up store and display layouts. Also at Reebok, Jenn and other designers printed and cut out paper team logos to pin on sample garments to check size and placement of the graphic before requesting a prototype from the factory. Early phase designs of air traffic control devices have been tested for controller and pilot responses using screen displays drawn on paper.

JCPenney is an example of what happens when a company neglects to check for meaningful and joyful essence beforehand. During the winter of 2012, when Ron Johnson was CEO, JCPenney ran a television ad announcing the elimination of frequent sales and the banishing of the sales brochures. The ad showed people overwhelmed by sale ads spilling out of mailboxes, constantly clipping ads from newspaper flyers, continually looking at shop window ads, and always seeing sale banners in stores. The people screamed "Noooooooooooo!" from the stress of being besieged by all the sale ads. The ad ended with the words, "ENOUGH. IS. ENOUGH." Many comments were posted online by JCPenney customers saying that they found the screams in the ad upsetting. Thus the ad, which intended to say that JCPenney would stop irritating customers with frequent sales, was itself annoying.

Johnson also came up with a new pricing strategy, rounding up prices ending in 99 cents to whole dollars. According to Brad Tuttle, writing for *Time,* Johnson was asked about testing the new pricing strategy before it was implemented, and he "reportedly shot down the idea, responding, 'We didn't test at Apple.'"[3] Jobs didn't believe in asking customers about their reactions to Apple products, but he seemed to have an innate sense of what would appeal to customers, so he got away with it. But most people don't have the sense that Jobs had, so testing or viewing from the customer's perspective is usually advantageous.

In hindsight it's evident that Johnson's changes weren't vetted from the perspectives of existing or potential customers. Johnson likely thought he was simplifying the customer experience. But his changes, unfortunately, were not meaningful and joyful to JCPenney's customers.

In his consulting practice Jim tries out various ways to add flair to his analyses, reports, and briefings for audiences and clients, but in non-threatening situations where there will be little consequence if the flair doesn't work. He's been intrigued by the online offerings of the company Despair, Inc.[4] Despair sells what it calls Demotivators, which are parodies of classic traditional motivational posters. For example, one Despair poster features a picture of a sunset over a beach with the words, "If a pretty poster and a cute saying are all it takes to motivate you, you probably have a very easy job. The kind robots will be doing soon." A poster concerned with meetings has a picture of overlapping hands from several people and the expression, "None of us is as dumb as all of us."

Jim purchased card-sized versions of many Despair demotivating posters to hand out at sessions he taught or facilitated, to provide some levity. The first time Jim taught his one-and-a-half-day course on how to conduct benefit assessments for new technology, he put a Despair card at all the students' places during lunch so they would see them upon return. Jim thought they would realize that the cards were making fun of the motivational posters that were, perhaps, hanging around their offices, and they would have a

light laugh before continuing with the workshop. But upon returning from lunch the attendees looked at the cards with puzzled ex-
pressions and asked what the handouts were. They weren't offended by the cards; they just didn't understand their purpose. So Jim
quickly moved to collect them. The course went on with no further
mention of the cards, the attendees continued to pay attention, and
the course received positive ratings. Nothing negative happened
because of this misguided attempt at flair. But it also didn't succeed
because it wasn't sincere to the course. Lesson learned.

On July 3, 1956, Elvis Presley boarded a train in New York City
headed for Chattanooga, Tennessee. He had just finished his first
recording session for RCA Records. When the session was completed, producers and musicians sat in the studio and listened to
"Hound Dog," "Don't Be Cruel," and "Anyway You Want Me" over
the studio's fourteen-inch speaker. Everyone was satisfied. Well, almost everyone. In his roomette on the train, Presley plugged a portable record player with a tiny speaker into the electrical outlet. He
played acetate demos of his songs. That's how Alfred Wertheimer,
a photographer hired by RCA, found the young singer. Why, Wertheimer asked, was Presley listening to the songs on the tiny record
player when he had just heard them in the studio on a large speaker. "Oh, that's . . . the way my fans hear it, and that's the way I want
to hear it," Presley explained. "He listened to it over and over and
over again," Wertheimer said.[5] Elvis knew that the essence of his
recording effort was how the songs would sound to his fans when
played the way they would listen to them. While it was important
to have a catchy lyric, a captivating musical composition, and tal-
ented musicians, none of that mattered if the song didn't work in
the real world on that tiny portable record player.

Can the Flair Be Added Practically?

Besides validating that the flair makes your offering's essence meaningful and joyful, it also needs to be practical – can you feasibly incorporate the flair in your offering and keep the cost of adding it low enough that you can sell the offering at an acceptable price? Let's look at what some companies do to validate the cost, time, and logistics of adding flair.

When Reebok designers complete their design sketches, and before an item reaches the production phase, technical designers analyze construction details and specify the placement of seams and trims and the size and placement of graphics. Technical designers, measurement specialists, and product developers confer with the designers on making changes necessary for the garment to be actually manufactured and worn. After the team decides on a wearable and producible design, sourcing specialists locate vendors and manufacturers, and the developers communicate with factories to get prototypes produced and costs determined. No matter how innovative and exciting a new concept may be, it won't make it into stores if it can't meet budget or be constructed correctly. On the flip side, a garment that's under budget or easy to produce won't sell if the design isn't fresh and exciting.

The different Reebok teams, with their various fields of expertise, give input on each garment, and open communication is maintained to constantly review and revise designs through the months of prototyping. When budget or other limitations dictate simplification of a design idea, everyone makes suggestions as to what details can be altered to save costs and still reflect the original design concept. For instance, a factory may determine that the cost to manufacture an NHL fan hoodie is over budget and suggest removing the graphic on the shoulder to reduce cost. But designers may feel the shoulder graphic has a strong impact when the game is aired on television and is key to telling the team's visual story. Development and technical design may then suggest simplifying the hood shape, changing the fabric, or making the shoulder graphic using an alternative ink. After considering a variety of solutions, the team revises the hoodie to meet budget and keep the flair that's important to the offering's essence.

Reebok's Dominique Fillion explained that the neon green trim on the NHL clothing was a feasible, low cost, and meaningful way to add flair to the collection. Reebok buys trim in bulk for one collection, so using the neck tape across all tops in the NHL performance line makes it cheaper per unit. Also, the green stitching on the eyelet in the pocket for headphone access has a visual impact but little impact on production costs. Adding a tag on the in-shop garment that highlights this pocket eyelet as media access enhances the performance story, and using the same green on the in-store displays strengthens the brand's essence. The added cost of these was determined to be small for the benefit they provided.

When Lyons/Zaremba meets with clients, engineers, construction experts, and maintenance personnel to plan the strategy for designing an exhibit, the budget is always kept in mind. President Steve Lenox said he asks the team: "Do we have room for all the content you want to have? Do we have sufficient opportunities for people to have hands-on interactivity? And do we have gaps – can we add something here or there that will add another thing?" Content is designed to ensure that the exhibit will be cost-effective and, at the same time, retain the most benefit for the audience. The desired stories are edited, Lenox noted, to be the most beneficial mix of experiences given the budget. Lyons/Zaremba begins cost estimating and modeling early. "We don't know how much the annual operating cost will be," said Lenox, "but we ballpark a cost element, maybe $30,000 for a particular element."

Lyons/Zaremba also has to consider whether an exhibit design is practical for the client to maintain. Can the client get in and clean all parts of the exhibition area? Does the client clean windows by tipping them open or come down on a bosun's chair off the roof? If all logistics are considered up front as well as throughout the design and development process, there should be no surprises come installation and opening day.

The validation of the work Jim did for the Safe Flight 21 Cost-Benefit Subgroup wasn't about budget or timelines, but whether data could be obtained to calculate the measures. The availability of necessary data was validated by reviewing past benefit studies, talking to aviation experts, and meeting with the staff designing the data collection.

Practical issues of cost and the ability to produce the proposed flair must be considered throughout the design and development process. Sometimes aspects need to be modified or eliminated. So before totally abandoning a flair idea because it's not practical, try to generate other ideas or modifications that are more practical.

What Negative Reactions Might the Flair Prompt?

Customers' primary negative reactions to Tropicana's 2009 redesign of its orange juice carton, which replaced the orange-with-straw image with a glass-of-orange-juice image, were that the new image made Tropicana no longer seem notable compared to other brands and that Tropicana cartons were now hard to locate on the grocery store shelf. When sales of orange juice dropped 20 percent over a two-month period, Tropicana quickly went back to the original image. Conducting tests of the new carton in a few supermarkets, or trying it out with focus groups, might have given Tropicana pertinent feedback on its new design.

Lands' End, the clothing retailer known for conservative casual clothing, began a promotion in 2014 that rewarded its best customers with a bonus – a gift subscription to a magazine published by Condé Nast, such as *Vogue, Glamour,* and *Self.* Then *GQ* magazine was sent to customers. *The New York Times* reported, "But when the July issue of *GQ* landed in mailboxes across the country, the cover model was not wearing a monogrammed oxford or polar fleece. Instead, she was topless except for a strategically placed white flower lei. And some of the company's shoppers were none too pleased."[6] Dozens of complaints appeared on the Lands' End Facebook page. *The New York Times* reported comments that included: "My fourteen-year-old son brought in the mail today & was quite disturbed & fascinated by a 'gift' Lands' End sent us – a copy of GQ magazine with an absolutely OBSCENE cover!!!" and "We received your 'Lands' End Bonus' of GQ magazine this weekend, and we are absolutely horrified."

Edgar Huber, the chief executive of Lands' End, wrote an apologetic email to customers that included, "There are simply no excuses; this was a mistake." Lands' End changed the bonus from *GQ* to the Condé Nast *Traveler* magazine. However, Huber also stated in his email that GQ, a men's magazine, had been sent "since we did not want to exclude our male customers." *The New York Times* went on to report that this comment offended some customers: "'I think I was even more appalled at the excuse in the form of an apology that I was sent,' one woman wrote on the Facebook page. 'That they meant it to be a gift to their male customers. That is absolutely disgusting and a major disrespect to your female customers. Those types of magazines are degrading and make women out to be objects. If that is the type of mind-set your marketing has on women, then I think that person needs to be fired.'" In this case it's most likely that Lands' End didn't check the cover and contents of the GQ magazine that would be sent to customers.

Check the Flair and Be Prepared to Act

Check that your flair makes the essence of your offering meaningful and joyful, can be practically added to the offering and be produced cost-effectively, and will generate positive reactions. Sometimes the reaction to the flair can be unexpected and can't be detected in any validation and testing efforts. So be prepared to take action in response to any adverse reactions, including redesigning or removing the flair.

Essentials: Validate That the Flair Is Effective

- Validate your flair.

- Three types of validation for flair:

  - Is the flair effective (that is, does it make your offering meaningful and joyful)?

  - Can the flair be added practically?

  - What negative reactions might the flair prompt?

- To validate flair, ask:

  - What response does the flair evoke?

  - Is this a desired response?

  - Can the flair be incorporated into the offering?

  - Can the flair be manufactured or produced?

  - How might the flair be misinterpreted?

- To examine the effectiveness of flair:

  - When brainstorming to identify flair elements, examine the ideas from the perspective of potential customers.

  - Ask others in your company or outside your company for their reactions to the flair.

  - Examine flair ideas using mock-ups of its actual form.

- Get feedback from customers:

  - Design and conduct focus groups to elicit dialog on the flair.

  - Probe to understand answers.

  - Analyze feedback (such as looking at the spread or clustering of preferences).

  - Observe customer behavior.

  - Give samples to customers and elicit feedback.

12

Iterate Among Defining Essence, Adding Flair, and Validating Flair

You see how it is: the method must be absolutely practical,
reasonable, realistic, but the aim, the whole, the conception
is an eternal poem.

— Tomas Masaryk, President of Czechoslovakia
after World War I, speaking about the
country developing as a democracy

THE PEOPLE WE INTERVIEWED about how they and their teams create effective flair in products, services, or daily work didn't explicitly follow the steps we spelled out in chapters nine through eleven, one by one, in that order, and then declare themselves done. Rather, they iterated among the steps from conception to launch.

Iterate to Create Effective Flair

Fresh Tilled Soil, located in Watertown, Massachusetts, designs user experiences (UX) and interfaces for websites and mobile applications for a variety of clients. We've attended events held by

Fresh Tilled Soil, such as its annual UX Fests, where speakers from inside and outside the company talk about user experience and interface design. We also interviewed Richard Banfield, co-founder and CEO, about Fresh Tilled Soil's design process.

Banfield takes a broad view of flair, which includes the reputation of the company with the offering, the experiences of users, and the design of the offering. While discussing the merits of using a structured process to design flair, Banfield stated: "It's a little counter-intuitive because I think people think of flair as being somewhat of a loose-cannon creative process. They imagine that some creative people are getting lost in their own heads. Even our clients sometimes misunderstand the creative process. They think that a bunch of tattooed people with weird piercings go into a room, maybe indulge in some pharmaceuticals. And after a couple of weeks they come away with some wonderfully creative ideas. And that is exactly the opposite of what creativity is."

Banfield was educated as a microbiologist before becoming a designer and CEO, so Fresh Tilled Soil uses methodical approaches derived from his science background. Trial and error is part of his UX design process, as is taking care of details by testing and modifying. Fresh Tilled Soil's design steps, as described by Banfield, are:

1. Understand – Discuss with the client and do research to understand the problem.

2. Divergence (or Ideation) – Brainstorm and generate solutions.

3. Select Solutions – Decide which may work the best.

4. Prototype – Build the selected solutions.

5. Validate – Prove the ideas are workable and test with end-users for desired results.

These steps are conducted in short iterations of a week or two; repeating over a short timeframe enables the company to gain and apply new information at all steps. Ideas are checked and validated at each stage, with a thorough internal and external examination in Step 5. Banfield commented that some companies may have Steve Jobs's approach of not asking customers about products, but he recognizes that Jobs had a unique ability to empathize with customers. While Banfield views empathy as the most important quality of a good designer, he stressed the importance of always going through product testing and validation, including with customers, to ensure accurate results before launching.

One way Fresh Tilled Soil addresses the "wow factor" is to conduct early-stage validation interviews with potential users to obtain qualitative feedback on emotional reactions. This emotional content is merged with general best-practice modeling about how people behave and what their habit-forming routine might be. The company draws upon the work of researchers, such as B.J. Fogg, founder and director of the Persuasive Tech Lab at Stanford University, whose approach is: (1) Get specific – What behavior do you want? (2) Make it easy – How can you make the behavior easy to do? and (3) Trigger the behavior – What will prompt the behavior?[1]

If inconsistencies or incongruities are noticed between what's heard and what's generally understood as best practices, the anomaly is investigated. If it's a good anomaly it's left alone. When it's a bad anomaly, such as an outlier or something that's going to be negative for product development, it's addressed. Creating wow factors comes from finding what excites users. Certain Fresh Tilled Soil designs aren't intended to excite outright, since they might be created for business-to-business marketing, compliance applications, or healthcare applications. But the company does ensure that users are emotionally engaged. Banfield commented that sometimes the worst part of using a piece of technology is the anxiety it causes and that adding flair is about reducing this anxiety. Flair isn't always about increasing positive feelings; sometimes it's about decreasing negative feelings.

Fresh Tilled Soil used its structured approach to create a website for FitOrbit. FitOrbit uses the Internet to connect people who want to gain better health through exercise and nutrition with trainers, nutritionists, and other health-related professionals. Banfield thought of FitOrbit as a match.com for health. Customers complete an online profile and answer questions about desired results and program pace. They're paired with appropriate professionals who can help them meet their specific health and fitness goals. The matched health providers provide support to the customers online.

Fresh Tilled Soil worked closely with FitOrbit to understand the issues of connecting those seeking support and those providing it. What Fresh Tilled Soil found in its understand step was unexpected and provided the core of not only the web application design but of the offering that FitOrbit ended up embracing. The understand step found that customers were generally middle-aged women who felt dissatisfied with their weight, fitness, and level of activity. They were looking to find not just people who could help them with fitness and training but who would also be supporters and companions during their improvement process. Banfield described how Fresh Tilled Soil interpreted the results of this step: "We would explain it to ourselves saying it takes one person to gain weight or get unfit but takes two people to get fit or back in shape. Now that is critical. It's not about the particulars of the diet plan or the exercise plan; it's the particular relationship that you are in. And that allowed them to do amazing things." The company used this insight as an internal expression of the essence of FitOrbit to guide the website-design activities.

Fresh Tilled Soil developed their understanding of the customer's desire for empathy from a health provider by having extensive and probing conversations (the term interviews doesn't convey the personal nature of the exchanges) with customers. Banfield described sitting customers down and having a conversation around a series of "what" and "why" questions, such as: What are you looking for? – Be fit and lose weight; Why do you not go to the gym? – People at the gym are already fit and trainers can seem like drill sergeants; What will make you feel good about yourself? – Being healthy and having companionship now that the kids have grown and left.

These conversations with potential customers provided the insight for the wow factor: that the customer need wasn't solely about finding a professional with required skills but, even more importantly, about finding someone who could provide empathy and support to help the customer through the process. A professional who could provide both these qualities was the correct match.

Fresh Tilled Soil worked with FitOrbit to find a web-based solution that connected customers with skilled, empathetic support. Recognizing that someone seeking this support would probably be anxious using a match process on the Internet, the companies developed three channels, with varying comfort levels, for customers to find help: (1) a quick, check-box process for those who just want a straightforward way to find a match by entering desired support attributes, (2) a medium-paced process, and (3) a slow, guided process for hesitant customers. If customers are anxious about the process they can answer questions one at a time and slowly develop the match attributes that make them comfortable. The slow entry process focuses not so much on the particulars of a diet plan or fitness regimen but on the relationship between customer and fitness professional. To ensure that providers can deliver the needed companionship, prospective trainers and nutritionists complete a questionnaire, provide information about their training styles and skills, and are prescreened by FitOrbit. The resulting FitOrbit offering allows hesitant customers and their matched supporters to do amazing things. A meaningful and joyful essence – "health improvement support with an empathetic companion" – was achieved.

The depth of the emotional connections between the customers and fitness professionals was seen in customers' reactions to meeting their support providers in person for the first time. For FitOrbit commercials, customers were recorded while they told their personal stories about how they got in shape and about their fitness support and companionship. During this recording the customer's personal trainer walked on stage, and the two met in person for the first time. The meetings proved to be intensely emotional. "Imagine you've been working with someone for six months," Banfield said in describing the meeting, "and you've achieved all this success with them, and they've been part of the process and an advocate and supporter throughout the process, and suddenly while you're giving your video testimonial that person walks on stage and meets you for the first time. It's like an Oprah moment!"

All SEESEE elements of flair are present in the FitOrbit business strategy and customer-provider connection website. Fresh Tilled Soil built on the stories gathered from potential customers during the research phase when customers were asked a series of "why" questions regarding their desires and anxieties. Once customers' internal dialogs were understood, an external *story* of what FitOrbit could do was formulated to create a solution. The new FitOrbit business model and the new website offering provide an agreeable *experience*; the customers are *entertained* while engaged with their fitness supporters and routines; the offering is *sincere* to what customers seek in companionship; it's *excellent* with its three options for finding a fitness support match and with that match providing empathetic and skilled supporters; and it's *energizing* for the customers through their relationships and successes.

Tips for Creating Effective Flair

Almost any structured approach can be enhanced by discovering what works and what doesn't. Below are a few tips we gathered during our research for this book.

Iterate Among Flair Design Steps

Fresh Tilled Soil's Richard Banfield emphasized iterating among design steps, learning something new at each step and applying that new information throughout the iteration process. He said the company conducts the steps over a short period of time, say a week or two, so that necessary changes could be implemented quickly when repeating the steps. Ideas are checked and validated after each iteration as the design progresses.

Lyons/Zaremba and Reebok also iterate among their design steps. Initial design ideas may only provide partial solutions, and looking at all steps during each phase of the design and development process helps to flesh out the work as it progresses. Once the work is more fully developed, iterating helps refine solutions so that they're effective and practical.

Start Parts of Flair Design Early

Iterating among the first three steps in creating effective flair – defining the meaningful and joyful essence, adding the flair, and validating the flair – means that, besides defining the essence, some aspects of ideation and validation can begin early. The early validation activities used by Fresh Tilled Soil were mainly focused on potential customer interactions with the FitOrbit website. For some designs, cost considerations may be particularly important and should be addressed early on. Lyons/Zaremba discusses cost estimating early in their design timeline. This is particularly important in exhibit design work since the costs of individual displays and components can mount up when the whole exhibit space is considered. Steve Lenox said that he ballparks a cost element early and refines the estimate as design details evolve. With early cost estimates, desired visitor experiences can be changed to fit the budget.

Sweat the Details

During our interview at Fresh Tilled Soil, Richard Banfield said, "It's really, really important that you focus on lots of tiny little details to bring through an overall positive experience." The company addresses the small details in development through incremental testing and modifying, and by having clients participate in evaluating the details and any necessary solutions. Customers are continually apprised of what's being done, and their opinions are solicited. Customers are not asked if they like something, but rather: "Does this achieve the goals set out by the project? Does this enhance your brand?" Besides addressing details in the designs for clients, Fresh Tilled Soil considers details in its internal workings for quality, productivity, and public activities meant to build relationships with other industry professionals. Such efforts include an annual UX Fest for user experience design professionals, email notices of weekly podcast discussions with UX professionals, a stellar office layout, tables custom-built with wood reclaimed from submergence in fresh water, and an interactive digital greeting at the entrance for visitors. Banfield stated that doing all this "requires you to take care of lots of little details. . . . Nothing is left to chance."

Keep Your Eyes on the Prize

Occasionally ideas for flair may come so quickly that you try to put too many of them into one design. For each idea ask how it will enhance the customers' experience, and keep only the strongest. A clutter of unnecessary or flashy details in a design creates a muddled mess that's hard for the customer to understand or appreciate.

In the early 2000s the pharmaceutical group Eli Lilly and Company decided to build a new process to provide rapidly changing drug product information to salespeople that would replace the slow and expensive mailing of information. An information technology consulting firm hired to build the system designed a process that focused on maximizing the capabilities offered by the information technology rather than the needs of the business. As a consequence the system development was expensive and unnecessarily complex. An internal Lilly team eventually took over and worked with the sales staff to analyze what the new process should do without providing more functionality than necessary. The internally developed system was used successfully by Lilly.

No matter how innovative your flair ideas may seem, be prepared to scrap them if they don't enhance the user's experience. It's the customer, not you, who should fall in love with the flair.

. . .

In Part III you learned how to define the meaningful and joyful essence of your offering, how to add flair to achieve the meaningful and joyful essence of your offering, how to validate that the flair is effective, and how to iterate among these steps. In Part IV you'll learn various techniques for creating effective flair within the context of SEESEE and how to have fun with flair.

Essentials: Iterate Among Defining Essence, Adding Flair, and Validating Flair

- ■ Iterate among the steps to create flair.
- ■ Start various parts of flair design early.
- ■ Sweat the details.
- ■ Keep your eyes on the prize.

Miscellaneous Thoughts about Flair

13

Specific Techniques for Creating Effective Flair

There are tricks in every trade.

— Proverb

THERE ARE MANY, MORE-SPECIFIC TECHNIQUES to help you create effective flair within the context of SEESEE (story, entertainment, experience, sincerity, excellence, and energy). These include using humor and whimsy, enhancing reality, applying new technologies, using props, incorporating details, developing a signature style, providing premium offerings, taking a unique perspective, adding small touches of flair, and providing an enticing atmosphere.

Engage Audiences Using Humor and Whimsy

Humor in presentations engages the audience and helps them to remember your talk, and it's most effective if it's *sincere* to your topic and to the specific part of your talk where you use it. Use humor throughout your talk to hold the audience's interest.

One way to create humor is to adapt jokes that you've heard. Jim recently heard comedian Don Novello on SiriusXM's *Laugh USA*. Novello, who often performs as the fictional character Father Guido Sarducci, gave his Five Minute University sketch – in five minutes a student learns what the typical college graduate remembers five years after college.[1] If the student takes Spanish, Sarducci's university will only teach how to say in Spanish, "How are you?" and "Very well," since that's all they'll remember five years later. For business, the student will learn that one "buys something and sells it for more."

Jim thought that adapting Sarducci's comedy routine would be an effective way to present the summaries at the end of short courses he teaches. He describes Sarducci's Five Minute University routine and then presents a summary of his own talk, calling it the five-minute university on whatever his course topic is. This sketch has been effective in revitalizing the audience at the end of a talk and always evokes a few laughs.

One of Jim's favorite uses of humor in a presentation comes from Jack Levy, a friend from Pasadena High School in California. Levy describes taking a picture of a truck loaded with hay leaving Needles, California, while it passed a sign that said Needles. He showed this picture during a talk to butterfly enthusiasts about the difficulty in locating a hard-to-find butterfly in California and received a positive response from the audience. They particularly enjoyed the title Levy gave the picture, "Haystack in Needles," a play on "Needle in a Haystack." When Levy tells his story of creating the picture, even more humor is added to the narrative.

While humor is often an effective way to engage people, it can become boring if the same comic element is used over and over. In a 1990s version of Microsoft Windows, an animated paper clip with a smiling face (known as Clippy) would appear at the top of the screen to ask if the user wanted help. The first time Jim saw the paper clip he thought that it was clever and funny. The second and third times he smiled again, thinking it was witty. But he soon tired of seeing Clippy, which he now rarely clicked, and eventually he turned it off. Microsoft eliminated the paper clip from following versions of Windows.

Whimsy, which is related to playfulness, fancifulness, or cleverness, is more suited to repeated exposure than humor. For example, many people have purchased Michael Graves's teakettle with the whistling bird on the spout, which provides an on-going source of amusement.

Enhance Reality

Altering "reality" can provide flair.

Beats by Dr. Dre headphones achieved accolades by emphasizing the energetic driving bass beat of rock, hip-hop, and pop music. Other high-end headphones produced sound evenly across the music spectrum, which didn't provide the drama of Beats, which emphasized one part of the sound, the bass, increasing the impact of the music.

Kodak spent decades on research to improve the way its film replicated the colors in the real world. Fujifilm, however, introduced color film that enhanced natural colors for a more intense and deeper hue. This appealed to many people who liked more vibrant colors in their photographs.

Apply New Technologies

Keeping up with innovations in your own industry and in other fields can yield sources of flair. If you're inspired to add flair with new technology or other innovations, make sure it's relevant to your mission and is excellent.

Some corporations excite customers by using technological advancements in their products. For example, adidas spends considerable time and money researching technological advancements applicable to sportswear and athletic equipment. The head of adidas Sports Licensed Design, Boris Esterkes, said during our interview with him that he is always thinking about how to apply innovations in the athletic wear market. To avoid being a "me too" company, explained Esterkes, one must challenge what's currently happening in design and take risks, often launching something not previously seen on the market.

Esterkes described how adidas revolutionized football uniforms by capitalizing on a new seamless knitting technology – the jersey is now knit in one tubular piece. The jersey also has so much stretch that it clings to the body yet allows for a full range of mobility. This concept for a snug-fitting, stretchy, seamless jersey was meant to unite the uniform with the player, as if it were an extension of the body. "[The] football players needed something that would make them feel 'locked and loaded,'" Esterkes noted, a phrase that became adidas's marketing story for this new uniform. Zones of compression and ventilation were engineered at strategic points on the jersey that enhanced the connection between uniform and player. The look is smooth, iconic, and recognizable. After the sleek new uniform hit football fields, bloggers expounded and fans chatted online about the new look. Esterkes noted that these advanced, fitted uniforms quickly became a favorite of players and propelled the story of the adidas brand as a leader in sportswear.

Use Props

Props can be used to make a point and, at the same time, be entertaining. Often Jim wears ties that relate to the topic of his talk, workshop, or course. One tie has upside-down top hats, some of which have a rabbit coming out and some of which are empty. This is used for courses on benefit-cost assessment, where Jim explains that the students, when performing benefit analysis, can claim any benefit supported by their concepts and not just the target benefit. The hats with and without rabbits imply that they should look for benefits everywhere; sometimes they'll find some and sometimes they won't. For talks on project portfolio management, where decision-making information is defined for selecting which projects to fund, Jim wears a tie with pictures of jugglers; the tie represents juggling the various criteria for selecting which projects to fund. Audience members come up to Jim during breaks to look at his ties and discuss their meanings.

Richard Feynman, a Nobel Prize laureate and physics professor at the California Institute of Technology, demonstrated during a Senate hearing the inflexibility of frozen O-rings, which caused the NASA Space Shuttle orbiter Challenger disaster in 1986.[2] He put a clamp on an O-ring and submerged it in ice water. When he removed the O-ring from the ice water, the dent from the clamp remained and the O-ring was rigid. He *showed* that the O-ring had lost its flexibility, and its ability to seal, much more clearly and dramatically than the hearing's verbal testimony had.

Incorporate Details

An occasional detailed dive into some aspect of an offering can change the pace, heighten interest, and concretize the concepts being presented. Too much detail can overwhelm or bore, but a sprinkling of it in the right places can help to maintain attention as well as give a feel for real-world applications.

Think of books you're familiar with from your childhood, such as the Babar or Tintin books. Author and illustrator Jean de Burnhoff scattered incredibly detailed, double-page spreads throughout his Babar books.[3] In *The Story of Babar,* one particularly spectacular double-page spread shows Babar driving his red roadster along a river through a valley.[4] There are fertile farm fields, fiery flowers, and verdant vegetation throughout the picture; farm animals scattered everywhere; a farmhouse and a distant village; and flying birds and insects. On the river are a tugboat towing a barge and a man fishing off a skiff. A hot air balloon, an airplane, and a train are in motion. You can't help but pause to look over the details of the intricate scene before resuming the narrative.

The Adventures of Tintin series of comic books, created by George Remi, a Belgian who wrote under the name Hergé, is another example where small drawings move the story along with an occasional large, detailed picture interspersed to refocus attention. The books feature Tintin, a young reporter, who becomes involved in a variety of adventures and solves mysteries set throughout the world. The books mostly feature typical small cartoon-style drawings, with many to a page as in a traditional comic book, that tell the story. Once in a while, though, there's a dramatic half-page illustration of a vast and elaborate scene. In *The Blue Lotus* a half-page drawing of a crowded urban Chinese street scene features detailed storefronts and overhead banners.[5] An abundantly detailed oceanfront illustration in *The Seven Crystal Balls* shows a cargo ship being loaded by a crane with stacks of freight on the dock.[6] These illustrations provide a change of pace for the viewer, who can pause from concentrating on Tintin's exciting adventures to absorb a grand scene.[7]

Jim intersperses an occasional deep dive in his presentations and reports to provide a change of pace in the continuous flow of information. In his short course on how to conduct benefit assessments he includes two in-depth examples, one on calculating safety benefits and the other on flight timesaving benefits. Both examples can be understood by audiences who haven't performed such assessments, yet they have enough detail to convey the calculations involved.

Develop a Signature Style

A personal, signature style with flair can make your offering stand out.

Boutique hotels began appearing in the 1980s, featuring themed, stylish décor and unique offerings. They're generally smaller than the traditional, big-brand hotels and emphasize comfortable and welcoming settings. Several large-hotel brands have started boutique hotel sub-brands to capitalize on this trend, which illustrates a way to extend offerings by using a signature style to add flair. For example, the Indigo and Aloft hotels are relatively new boutique hotels owned by the existing big-hotel brands Inter-Continental Hotels Group and Starwood Hotels & Resorts Worldwide, respectively. Guestrooms at Hotel Indigo feature murals, area rugs, duvets, and slipcovers that are changed periodically. The lobby and reception area reflect a particular season with music, artwork, murals and directional signage. Each Hotel Indigo property is designed to reflect the culture, character, and history of the surrounding neighborhood.[8, 9]

Aloft's signature style is to encourage socialization in the inviting public spaces, which are designed to draw guests from their rooms to meet other guests. Those staying at the hotel can read the paper, work on their laptops via hotel-wide Wi-Fi access, grab a drink with friends at the bar in the lobby area, and obtain food and beverages from the lobby area.[10] There are a variety of seating and table options in the lobby to suit work or social activities. The traditional reception desk has been replaced by a circular counter similar to a checkout counter at a store, giving the lobby a more open feel with easily accessible staff. Another signature spin is the hotel's use of the latest technology. Guestrooms feature a space that's a combination high-tech office and entertainment center. Some of the room amenities include wireless Internet access, one-stop connectivity for multiple electronic gadgets, and a ready link to hook up mobile devices to a large, flat panel LCD television for optimal sound and viewing.

Successful fashion designers, such as Coco Chanel, solidify their brands by always offering something new and exciting while consistently maintaining their unique brand identity. Even though their design directors have changed and fashions have evolved, the image of Chanel is recognizable all over the world with variations of its boucle suits and interlocking C logo.

Entertainers as well have successfully used personalized signature flair to maintain long careers. Madonna has enjoyed a 30-year celebrity status with a signature style in her attire, in her performances, and in her music videos, all of which incorporate flashy flair. Part of her signature style is to re-invent her image periodically, though you always know it's Madonna. Lady Gaga and Katy Perry are two more entertainers enjoying success by performing with flair and maintaining unique personal styles.

Malcolm Gladwell has become hugely successful with his books *The Tipping Point, Outliers, David and Goliath,* and others spending many months on bestseller lists. Gladwell writes about counterintuitive aspects of common things (such as Hush Puppies shoes, speed dating, and tennis players), and he tells engaging anecdotes about his topics. His subjects can be summarized by a quote from him, "There is more going on beneath the surface than we think, and more going on in little, finite moments of time than we would guess."[11] His unusual takes on common objects give his writing flair that engages large audiences.

Parsons School of Design placed great importance on developing a signature style when Jenn attended the school. In the course of her studies she was required to take a class called "Process and Skills," which was solely about building a unique brand, creating consistently styled presentation materials, and ensuring that all details were executed professionally. For a final project everyone in the class had to design a custom business card, a mailer, and a presentation folder that reflected their hypothetical eponymous fashion design brand. The excellence of the execution and design aesthetic were graded, but, more importantly, the students were judged on the uniqueness of the identity and the relevance to the style they wished to highlight. In Jenn's "Fashion Industry – Design" class, the students were required to design a take-away that was a clever handout to leave or mail after an interview that served as a thank you note and a reminder of the talent and personal style the candidate offered. Some results were beautiful postcards capturing the designer's eye for layout and color, paper dolls with cute original outfits, and accordion-folded handouts showcasing the designer's work. The fashion design program at Parsons culminated in a class called "Portfolio," which taught the students to build cohesive collections to show potential employers. Emphasizing ubiquitous excellence, part of each student's grade depended on their choice of an actual portfolio case. Students could purchase a case or craft one, but the objective was that its style reflect the designs held within and the designer's personal aesthetic – their signature style.

Provide Premium Offerings

Improving a product or service from existing bare-bones offerings can provide more opportunities for flair and for making more money. Your prices will likely be higher than your competitors' prices, but customers will often pay more for the improvements. Just look at Apple's command of premium prices with its design flair and customers' perception of better quality.

Starbucks is a classic example of a company that uses this strategy. Before Starbucks there were many options for getting a cup of coffee, such as coffee shops, donut stores, fast-food shops, and small convenience markets. Good quality coffee, however, was often lacking. Starbucks offered premium coffee, the experience of a barista brewing your coffee, and a pleasant setting – and created a zealous following. It charged more for the superior coffee and atmosphere, and people came. Having a strong company culture and products that were developed using tailored processes assured the necessary consistency.

Lululemon became successful selling stylish yoga clothes. A February 2015 *New Yorker* magazine article by Lizzie Widdicombe stated that the founder, Chip Wilson, had a vision: What if yoga clothes were so attractive women would want to wear them all day?[12] The yoga clothing launched by Lululemon was more expensive than other brands, but Wilson and his wife Shannon, a Lululemon designer, became billionaires. Since the company puts styling into its clothing, uses a now-iconic logo, and sells at premium prices, its yoga clothes have become a status symbol for celebrities and suburban moms, who wear them while running errands. Someone might have a whole Lululemon outfit and never attend a yoga class.

Take a Unique Perspective

Taking a unique perspective with your offering can also make your product, service, or daily work stand out.

Al Jacobson, working as an independent consultant, helped a supplier of shareholder recordkeeping systems write a contract proposal for an investment firm. The proposal was for the development of a state-of-the-art, computer-based recordkeeping system. Instead of describing how the work would be done, Jacobson wrote the proposal as if it were five years in the future, and the financial services firm had already installed and was using the new recordkeeping system. His proposal described how the financial services firm, following the nearly flawless execution of the proposed innovative services, had achieved a level of investor satisfaction and loyalty unprecedented in the investment industry. Jacobson presented an imaginary press release for the investment firm that described the investor success and awards received because the company installed the proposed shareholder system. The body of the proposal was written from the vantage point of the future, looking back to describe the work the supplier had done working with the financial services firm to develop and implement the new system.

The flair – a narrative proposal set in the future that described the successful state of the financial institution – worked. Jacobson's client succeeded in obtaining the work, and Jacobson received more consulting work from this client.

Add Small Touches of Flair

Small touches of flair can be inexpensive, yet that attention to detail can inspire customers, colleagues, and audiences.

Jim regularly patronizes the L.A. Burdick Chocolate Shop & Tea Room in Harvard Square. On a visit in March 2015 he observed a staffer arranging carpet runners to line up parallel with the floorboards. Jim mentioned this to the store manager, Fraser Currie, who said that Burdick intentionally pays attention to small details. He showed Jim how the staff fluffs ribbons on candy boxes and artistically arranges small candy bags on the shelves. Currie described observing an employee at the Burdick production site in Walpole, New Hampshire, hand chopping half-inch square chocolate chips from a thin sheet of chocolate to be placed in small bags to sell. For Currie this sight epitomized the care that Burdick puts into its products.

While moderating a panel discussion at a Harvard Business School Association of Boston event, professor Ben Shapiro used action to produce flair. Many speakers move from behind the lectern to be near the audience. Shapiro, however, walked up the aisles between the seat rows. This movement created a close rapport between the professor and the audience. Sometimes when he asked the panelists a question, he sat down in an audience seat to convey that this was the panelists' moment. This physical engagement with the audience enlivened the session and made it more memorable.

Provide an Enticing Atmosphere

An enticing atmosphere can add significant flair to an offering that will make a customer's experience memorable.

The Andover Shop, operated by Charlie Davidson in Harvard Square since 1953, sells Ivy League and British-influenced men's apparel with bright colors and intriguing fabrics (what Davidson calls surface interest). Jim interviewed Davidson over lunch in April 2015. The atmosphere of the Andover Shop is that of an informal club where "everyone knows your name." This quality, along with the styles offered, forms its appeal. During their lunch Davidson went to his store next door to greet a long-time customer who was picking up a sport coat after its alterations. This personal service is part of the store's essence. Another part is illustrated by Davidson's method of hiring employees. "[I] ask why they would like to work at the Andover Shop or if they have any questions," Davidson said. "If they ask about hours and benefits, I reject them. If they say they like clothing and talking with people, I hire them."

Jim and his wife Joanne fortuitously found the Bosie Tea Parlor in New York City's West Village while walking through the rain and looking for a place to sit and have a snack. When they entered they were engulfed by Bosie's warm and welcoming mix of modern and traditional décor. Particularly fetching were large, round, copper-colored tea tins on tiered shelves that covered three of the walls. The staff greeting was congenial and engaging. The offerings were extensive, including fifty-seven varieties of tea, each with a description of its taste and geographic origin.

Impressed by Bosie, Jim talked extensively with his server, Ben Frankenberg, about the tea parlor. Frankenberg said that word spread about the quality of Boise's macaroons and pastries, made by its own pastry chef, and Bosie began a sister wholesale business to provide these items to cafes and restaurants around the city. In an amusing conclusion to a delightful experience, Frankenberg brought the check inside the front cover of a book by E. B. White, *Here's New York*. He noted that occasionally people take the book with them, so Bosie continually buys more. The sincerely friendly and enthusiastic service, the subdued yet cute and cozy décor, the vast selection, and the quality of the pastries created a charming atmosphere.

There are other ways to add flair that we didn't discuss in this chapter. Our intention is to provide some ideas for you to build on to create flair, and we hope you'll be inspired to invent your own ways of adding flair.

Essentials: Specific Techniques for Creating Effective Flair

■ Tools you can use to add flair to your offering include:

- Humor and whimsy
- Enhanced reality
- New technology
- Props
- Varied details
- Signature style
- Premium offerings
- Unique perspective
- Small touches of flair
- Enticing atmosphere

14

Having Fun with Flair

Creative ideas flourish best in a shop which preserves some spirit of fun. Nobody is in business for fun, but that does not mean there cannot be fun in business.

— Leo Burnett, advertising executive

I N A *CALVIN AND HOBBES* COMIC STRIP that appeared on January 10, 2015, on the GoComics website, the little boy Calvin contemplates creativity.[1] In the first panel he says, "Why does man create?" In the second panel he says, "Is it man's purpose on earth to express himself, to bring form to thought, and to discover meaning in experience?" The third panel shows Calvin pondering. In the fourth panel he says, "Or is it just something to do when he's bored?" We don't think that creativity, particularly when designing flair, is just something to do when you're bored. As we'll show in this chapter, working with flair can be – and should be – fun.

Flair Should Be Fun!

Roger Ebert and Gene Siskel used to host a television show called *At the Movies,* where they reviewed newly released films. In one episode they described three criteria actor George C. Scott asserted for judging a great acting performance: (1) how the actor played the range of emotions, such as happiness, anger, disappointment, and despair; (2) if the actor seemed like the same person in all roles or appeared to subsume into different characters; and (3) how well the actor conveyed to the audience that he or she was having fun with the role. Notice that Scott included conveying joy in work as one of his three standards in judging an actor's performance.

Fun in creating and conveying flair is exemplified in the "60-second Super-cool Fold of the Week" videos that Trish Witkowski of Foldfactory.com posts on YouTube (see Exhibit 14.1).[2] Foldfactory.com provides ideas and support for folding direct mailings, brochures, pamphlets, flyers, and other printed materials. The services include custom folding templates, folding ideas and videos, folding resources, and specialized software services. Each week Witkowski,

Exhibit 14.1. Conveying flair with infectious fun, Trish Witkowski presents a Foldfactory.com "60-second Super-cool Fold of the Week."

who calls herself Chief Folding Fanatic at Foldfactory.com, creates and posts a 60-second video. She has done this for over five years, posting over 318 folds as of November 2015. The fold ideas are sent to her, usually by the printers or businesses that create them, and she then takes about 60 seconds to show the folded material, deconstruct it, and demonstrate how the fold was made. Her enthusiasm is infectious. She's clearly having fun in her videos. She wears a different t-shirt each week with a saying adapted to contain the word *fold*, such as: "Put your best fold forward," "Hit the ground folding," "One good fold deserves another," "Curses! Folded again," and "Have I got a fold for you!"

Around 1970 Jim was an applied mathematics Ph.D. student at Harvard University's School of Engineering and Applied Sciences. The professors and graduate students in optimal control theory gathered over lunch each Friday for an informal presentation by one of the group. Microcomputers and PowerPoint didn't exist, so viewgraph machines were used to project what was written or drawn on letter-sized, clear plastic transparent sheets. In one memorable talk graduate student Alan Starr projected a transparency with a diagram. Then he flipped another transparency on top of the original transparency to add more detail to the diagram. Jim and the others had never seen this effect before, and there was oohing and aahing and smiles in the audience. This "fold-over" seems oddly primitive and strange today, but it was new then. At a later session Starr used three fold-overs, and later, four fold-overs. The audience laughed upon seeing each of these, and Starr also smiled since he knew this was fun for everyone. (Years later Jim found out that the fold-overs were the inspiration of Professor Yu-Chi "Larry" Ho, Starr's and Jim's Ph.D. thesis advisor.)

At the Reebok design reviews Jenn attended, the apparel designers began to step up the level of flair in their presentations by adding props, creating beautifully crafted handouts, and incorporating audience participation to capture the essence of the new styles they were pitching. For a vintage-inspired collection of throwback hoodies and t-shirts, the printed handouts were hand-bound in canvas that the designers had stained, sanded, and distressed to convey a retro feeling. Another designer presenting traditional fan gear t-shirts and jackets passed out cracker jacks and peanuts to snack on during his review, in order to capture the audience's attention and evoke the joy of being at a sporting event. Several years later these routine meetings still stand out in Jenn's mind as a fun and informative time for all involved, and she can clearly remember the essence of each design collection.

Adding effective flair is work and needs to be taken seriously, but it can be fun since you're dealing with the emotions of customers, colleagues, or audiences. Working with flair will be a change of pace from your other daily activities, and it's interesting to look for and note appealing designs as you go through your day. You'll likely feel pleased when you think up a promising idea for flair. Other aspects of working with flair that are enjoyable are learning new skills to create flair, surveying other fields to learn techniques and principles that you can adapt, and appreciating the reactions of others as they're energized by your flair and influenced to act.

Essentials: Having Fun with Flair

- Flair is fun to create. It:
  - Adds enjoyment to your workday
  - Provides a change of pace from your other daily activities
  - Expands your skill set through learning new approaches to create flair
  - Expands your horizon through surveying other fields related to flair
  - Provides gratification when you see others energized by your flair and influenced to act

15

In Conclusion: One Final Example of Discovering an Essence

Granting myself permission to use my innate skills of the heart, accepting that emotion was perfectly valid in the art of persuasion, amounted to nothing less than a breakthrough.

— Sonia Sotomayor, Associate Justice of the Supreme Court of the United States

DISCOVERING THE ESSENCE OF YOUR WORK can enhance your effectiveness. For our final word on essence and flair we'll recount the experience of Sonia Sotomayor, Associate Justice of the Supreme Court of the United States, who learned to include emotion in her appeals to juries when she was a New York County Assistant District Attorney.

In her memoir, *My Beloved World,* Sotomayor recounts her first job after Yale Law School as an Assistant District Attorney in New York City.[1] Shortly after she began working in felony trials, she prosecuted the same defendant in two different trials back-to-back. Sotomayor felt her cases were solid, but she lost both times to an experienced defense attorney from Legal Aid. She couldn't figure out why she had lost the cases, so she went to her bureau chief, Warren Murray, for advice. After she explained her presentation of the two cases, "[Warren] identified the problem instantly: I was appealing to logic, not morality, and in effect letting the jury off the hook. Since it is painful to most jurors to vote 'guilty' and send a human being to jail, you couldn't simply reason with them to do it; you had to make them feel the necessity. 'They have to believe that they have a moral responsibility to convict,' Warren said. Even the most perfectly logical argument, absent passion, would make the choice seem like one of personal discretion rather than solemn duty."

Sotomayor considered this to be the most powerful lesson she would learn about trial skills. She changed her complete approach to addressing juries, from jury selection through formulating her summations. After adding emotional elements to her trial repertoire, she said that she never lost a case. She had a couple of hung juries and some convictions on fewer than all counts, but she never had another acquittal.

Sotomayor delineates an assortment of tactics she formulated to add emotional elements to her interactions with jurors. While the prosecutor usually has no need to establish a motive under the law, Sotomayor says: "'Why would she have done that?' is something we instinctively ask before we allow ourselves to conclude 'she did it.' The state's case is a narrative: the story of a crime. The defense has only to cast doubts on the coherence of that story. The 'why' elements of the story must make sense – what would have motivated this person to hurt that person – before you can engage the jurors' empathy, put them in the shoes of the accused or the victim, as needed." She goes on to say, "I learned to ask general questions so as to elicit details, with powerful sensory associations: the colors, the sounds, the smells that lodge an image in the mind."

Devising a case, she states, is a two-step process of building the strategy out of reason and logic and then throwing yourself into it heart and soul.

Sotomayor incorporated several of the SEESEE building blocks for flair in her redefined trial tactics that made them emotion-based as well as logic-based. Flair may not be the appropriate term for the criminal courtroom, but Sotomayer did create a style for presenting her cases that reflects the SEESEE elements. First, she emphasized telling the *story* of a crime. While not entertaining in a fun way, her method of questioning to evoke powerful sensory associations of colors, sounds, and smells to place an image in the jurors' minds involved elements one might employ to *entertain*. She created the *experience* for the jurors of what the victim was feeling. Certainly the emotions she elicited from the jurors were *sincere* to her prosecution case. Her careful trial preparation was *excellent* and presented the emotional and rational aspects of her case. And she was certainly trying to *energize* the jury to convict. Sotomayor's decision to involve a meaningful and, instead of joyful we'll say, emotional essence in her trial work resulted in such success that she thereafter never had an acquittal.

We hope this final example conveys the robust power of defining a meaningful and joyful essence for whatever your offering may be, along with the effectiveness of applying the SEESEE building blocks.

. . .

May you enjoy stellar success with your products, services, and daily work by incorporating flair built on a meaningful and joyful essence.

Essentials: One Final Example of Discovering an Essence

- Discovering the essence of what you're working on provides a deeper understanding and enables you to enhance your work.

NOTES

Chapter 1

1. Burt Helm, "How Dr. Dre's Headphones Company Became a Billion-Dollar Business," *Inc.* (May 2014), http://www.inc.com/audacious-companies/burt-helm/beats.html.
2. Mark Bergen, "Beats," *Advertising Age* (December 8, 2015): 16.
3. Burt Helm (see note 1).
4. Brian Solomon, "It's Official: Apple Adds Dr. Dre With $3 Billion Beats Deal," *Forbes* (May 28, 2014), http://www.forbes.com/sites/briansolomon/2014/05/28/apple-brings-dr-dre-on-board-with-official-3-billion-beats-deal/.
5. Jim Edwards, "Check Out The Insane Lengths Zappos Customer Service Reps Will Go To," *Business Insider* (January 9, 2012), http://www.businessinsider.com/zappos-customer-service-crm-2012-1.
6. Max Chafkin, "The Zappos Way of Managing," *Inc.* (May 1, 2009), http://www.inc.com/magazine/20090501/the-zappos-way-of-managing.html.
7. James La Barre, "Defining Service and Culture: The Zappos Model," *Beyond Marketing Blog* (April 8, 2013), http://blog.amazethecustomer.com/2013/04/08/defining-service-and-culture-the-zappos-model/.
8. Winter Nie and Beverley Lennox, "Case Study: Zappos," *Financial Times* (February 16, 2011), http://www.ft.com/cms/s/0/98240e90-39fc-11e0-a441-00144feabdc0.html#axzz3iRe63amG.
9. Jim heard Doris Kearns Goodwin discuss this approach to her recent biographies at a book talk sponsored by the Harvard Bookstore in Cambridge, Massachusetts, on November 13, 2013.
10. Stefanie Cohen, "Fourscore and 16,000 Books," *The Wall Street Journal* (October 12, 2012), http://www.wsj.com/articles/SB10000872396390444024204578044403434070838.

11. Sam Kashner, "The Class that Roared," *Vanity Fair* (March 2014): 372–81.

12. Walter Isaacson, *Steve Jobs* (New York: Simon & Schuster, 2011), 472.

13. International Data Corporation, "Worldwide Tablet Market Surges Ahead on Strong First Quarter Sales, Says IDC," *Reuters* (May 1, 2013), http://www.reuters.com/article/2013/05/01/ca-idc-idUSnBw016369a+100+BSW20130501.

14. Leo Sun, "Why Microsoft's Surface Pro 3 Sales Soared as Apple's iPad Sales Plunged," *The Motley Fool* (October 29, 2014), http://www.fool.com/investing/general/2014/10/29/why-microsofts-surface-pro-3-sales-soared-as-apple.aspx.

15. Phil Wahba, "Target Has a New CEO: Will He Re-Energize the Retailer?" *Fortune* (March 1, 2015), http://fortune.com/target-new-ceo/.

16. Brad Tuttle, "The 5 Big Mistakes That Led to Ron Johnson's Ouster at JC Penney," *Time* (April 9, 2013), http://business.time.com/2013/04/09/the-5-big-mistakes-that-led-to-ron-johnsons-ouster-at-jc-penney/.

17. Matthew Graham, "Dinner with the FT: Jay Leno," *Financial Times* (November 17, 2006), http://www.ft.com/intl/cms/s/0/909253c0-753a-11db-aea1-0000779e2340.html.

Chapter 2

1. Eliza E. Rathbone and George T. M. Shackelford, *Impressionist Still Life* (Washington, DC: The Phillips Collections/Harry N. Abrams, 2001), 65, 79.

2. *Frédéric Bazille: Prophet of Impressionism* (Montpellier, France, and Brooklyn, NY: The Brooklyn Museum, 1992), 114.

3. *Merriam-Webster Unabridged Collegiate Dictionary,* s.v. "essence," http://unabridged.merriam-webster.com/collegiate/essence.

4. *Consumer Reports: 2015 Annual Auto Issue* (April 2015), 58.

5. Jim Henry, "10 Most Expensive Cars of 2014: Keeping Up With The 1 Percent," *Forbes* (December 19, 2013), http://www.forbes.com/sites/jimhenry/2013/12/19/10-most-expensive-cars-for-2014-keeping-up-with-the-joneses/.

6. U.S. Department of Energy, "2015 Best and Worst Fuel Economy Vehicles," Fueleconomy.gov (May 28, 2015), https://www.fueleconomy. gov/feg/best-worst.shtml. Fuel efficiency is combined city/highway.

7. Stuart Elliott, "Tropicana Discovers Some Buyers Are Passionate About Packaging," *The New York Times* (February 23, 2009), http://www. nytimes.com/2009/02/23/business/media/23adcol.html.

8. Charlie Rose interview with Danny Meyer, New York City restaurateur and CEO of the Union Square Hospitality Group, "Charlie Rose Show," (April 19, 2012), http://charlierose.com/watch/60063696.

9. Justin Bachman, "Will a New CEO at JetBlue Mean More Fees and Higher Profit?" *Bloomberg Businessweek* (September 18, 2014), http:// www.businessweek.com/articles/2014-09-18/will-a-new-ceo-at-jetblue-mean-more-fees-and-higher-profits.

10. Daniel M. Hayborn, *Happiness: A Very Short Introduction* (Oxford, England: Oxford University Press, 2013), 54, 70–71.

11. Dylan Evans, *Emotion: A Very Short Introduction* (Oxford, England: Oxford University Press, 2001), 5, 27, 47.

12. Clayton M. Christensen, Scott Cook, and Taddy Hall, "Marketing Malpractice: The Cause and the Cure," *Harvard Business Review* (December 2005), https://hbr.org/2005/12/marketing-malpractice-the-cause-and-the-cure.

13. Kevin Bolen and Robyn Bolton, "Customer Solutions Using Jobs to Be Done," Innosight (December 3, 2012), https://www.youtube.com/watch?v=zToE0yYqp8k.

Chapter 3

1. Jim Wangers, *Glory Days: When Horsepower and Passion Ruled Detroit* (Cambridge, MA: Bentley Publishers, 1998), 43–52.

2. John Caples' "learn to play the piano" ad, annotated by Susanna Hutcheson, accessed on July 4, 2014, http://www.powerwriting.com/caples.html.

3. The Viral Nova website, run by Scott DeLong, assembles popular stories circulating on the web that are likely to engage readers emotionally. Accessed on July 7, 2014, http://www.viralnova.com/.

4. Caroline Moss, "This Ad From 1926 Is The Driving Force Behind Much Of The Internet's Viral Content," *Business Insider* (December 2, 2013), http://www.businessinsider.com/they-laughed-when-i-sat-down-at-the-piano-but-when-i-began-to-play-2013-12.

5. "John Caples," *Advertising Age* (March 29, 1999), http://adage.com/article/special-report-the-advertising-century/john-caples/140200/.

6. Tim Nudd, "Apple's 'Get a Mac,' The Complete Campaign," *Adweek* (April 13, 2011), http://www.adweek.com/adfreak/apples-get-mac-complete-campaign-130552.

7. "The Original and Complete Target Alouette TV Commercial," YouTube video, 0:54, posted by Tony Sandlin, March 12, 2012, http://www.youtube.com/watch?v=bK523_NoT70.

8. Stephen Denning, *The Springboard: How Storytelling Ignites Action in Knowledge-Era Organizations* (Boston: Butterworth-Heinemann, 2001), 9–16.

9. Jonathan Gottschall, *The Storytelling Animal: How Stories Make Us Human* (New York: First Mariner Books, 2013), 3–4.

10. Ibid., 5–6.

11. Ibid., 64.

12. Ibid., 137–38.

13. Chip Heath and Dan Heath, *Made to Stick: Why Some Ideas Take Hold and Others Come Unstuck* (London: Arrow Books/Random House, 2008), 16–18.

14. Stefan Mumaw, *Chasing the Monster Idea: The Marketer's Almanac for Predicting Idea Epicness* (Hoboken, NJ: John Wiley & Sons, 2011), 162–67.

15. Ian Parker, "The Real McKee," *The New Yorker* (October 20, 2003), http://www.newyorker.com/magazine/2003/10/20/the-real-mckee.

16. Robert McKee, *Story: Substance, Structure, Style, and the Principles of Screen Writing* (New York: Regan Book/HarperCollins, 1997), 19.

17. Chip Heath and Dan Heath (see chapter 3, note 13).

18. Mary Teresa Bitti, "How Pandora Jewellery Grew to Become a Mega Global Brand," *Financial Post* (January 22, 2014), http://business.

financialpost.com/entrepreneur/franchise-focus/how-pandora-jewellery-grew-to-become-a-mega-global-brand.

19. Beth Kowitt, "How Ikea Took Over the World," *Fortune* (March 15, 2015), http://fortune.com/ikea-world-domination/.

Chapter 4

1. William Shakespeare, *Macbeth,* Act 5, Scene 5.
2. *Bible,* King James Version, Gospel of John, Chapter 11, Verse 35.
3. *Merriam-Webster Unabridged Collegiate Dictionary,* s.v. "entertainment," http://unabridged.merriam-webster.com/collegiate/entertainment.
4. Peter G. Stromberg, *Caught in Play: How Entertainment Works on You* (Stanford, CA: Stanford University Press, 2009), 6, 13.
5. Thinkmap Visual Thesaurus, accessed August 29, 2014, http://www.visualthesaurus.com/.
6. *Merriam-Webster Unabridged Collegiate Thesaurus* (see note 3).

Chapter 5

1. *Merriam-Webster Unabridged Collegiate Dictionary,* s.v. "entertainment," http://unabridged.merriam-webster.com/collegiate/entertainment.
2. *Merriam-Webster Unabridged Collegiate Dictionary,* s.v. "experience," http://unabridged.merriam-webster.com/collegiate/experience.
3. Ibid.
4. Raymond Williams, *Keywords: A Vocabulary of Culture and Society* (Oxford, England: Oxford University Press, 2015), 84.
5. Walter Isaacson, *Steve Jobs* (New York: Simon & Schuster, 2011), 125–34.
6. Ken Segall, *Insanely Simple: The Obsession that Drives Apple's Success* (New York: Portfolio/Penguin, 2013), 3, 4.
7. Walter Isaacson (see note 5), 127.
8. Steve Krug, *Don't Make Me Think: A Common Sense Approach to Web Usability* (Berkeley, CA: New Riders, 2006).

9. *Samurai! Armor from the Ann and Gabriel Barbier-Mueller Collection,* Museum of Fine Arts, Boston, April 14, 2013, to August 4, 2013, http://www.mfa.org/exhibitions/samurai.

Chapter 6

1. *Merriam-Webster Unabridged Collegiate Dictionary,* s.v. "sincere," http://unabridged.merriam-webster.com/collegiate/sincere.
2. *Merriam-Webster Unabridged Collegiate Dictionary,* s.v. "genuineness," http://unabridged.merriam-webster.com/collegiate/genuineness.
3. *Merriam-Webster Unabridged Collegiate Dictionary,* s.v. "authentic," http://unabridged.merriam-webster.com/collegiate/authentic.
4. *Advertising Age* (July 8, 2002): 18.

Chapter 7

1. Paul Taylor, "Sony Smartwatch That Thinks Its Time Has Come," *Financial Times* (January 10, 2014): 10.
2. David Pogue, "A Watch That Sinks Under Its Features," *The New York Times* (October 2, 2014), http://www.nytimes.com/2013/10/03/technology/personaltech/samsung-watch-sinks-under-weight-of-its-features.html?
3. Jody Rosen, "The Apple Watch: More Than Just a Bracelet," *The New York Times* (May 5, 2015), http://tmagazine.blogs.nytimes.com/2015/05/05/apple-watch/?_r=0.
4. Trent Hamm, "The Netflix Culture of Excellence," *The Simple Dollar* (September 17, 2014), http://www.thesimpledollar.com/the-netflix-culture-of-excellence-and-how-to-capture-it-in-your-own-life/.
5. Emiliana Sandoval, "One Year: 2012 Fiat 500 Sport Verdict: Cute, But Looks Aren't Everything," *Motor Trend* (March 2013), http://www.motortrend.com/roadtests/oneyear/hatchbacks/1303_2012_fiat_500_sport_verdict/.
6. "2015 Fiat Hatchback Review," Edmunds.com, http://www.edmunds.com/fiat/500/2015/hatchback/review/.

7. "2015 Fiat 500: Reliability," *U.S. News & World Report: Best Cars,* http://usnews.rankingsandreviews.com/cars-trucks/FIAT_500/Reliability/.
8. *Consumer Reports New Car Preview 2015* (2014), 88.
9. Tobias Buck, "A Better Business Model," *Financial Times* (June 19, 2014): 7.

Chapter 8

1. Nancy Luna, "'Madness' in Texas as First 2 In-N-Out Restaurants Open," *The Orange County Register* (May 11, 2011; updated August 21, 2013), http://www.ocregister.com/articles/first-300116.
2. Nancy Luna, "Texas In-N-Out Restaurants to Open Wednesday," *The Orange County Register* (May 9, 2011; updated December 7, 2013), http://www.ocregister.com/articles/strong-592275-open-restaurant.html.
3. "Not-So-Secret Menu," In-N-Out Burger, http://www.in-n-out.com/menu/not-so-secret-menu.aspx.
4. *Merriam-Webster Unabridged Collegiate Dictionary,* s.v. "energy," http://unabridged.merriam-webster.com/collegiate/energy.
5. Kay Redfield Jamison, *Exuberance: The Passion for Life* (New York: Vintage Books, 2004), 138–39.
6. Rob Cross, Wayne Baker, and Andrew Parker, "What Creates Energy in Organizations?" *Sloan Management Review* 44, no. 4 (Summer 2003).
7. Geoff Herbert, "Customers Line Up for iPhone 6, iPhone Plus Outside the Apple Store in Syracuse," Syracuse.com (September 18, 2014; updated September 19, 2014), http://www.syracuse.com/news/index.ssf/2014/09/iphone_6_plus_line_apple_store_syracuse_destiny_usa.html.
8. Hiawatha Bray and Taryn Luna, "Consumers in Boston Get Their Hands on iPhone 6," *The Boston Globe* (September 19, 2014), http://www.bostonglobe.com/business/2014/09/19/consumers-boston-get-their-hands-iphone/B53GfEzSdujFxnJZqjQLPI/story.html.
9. Jonathan Phelps, "Sonic Barrier Broken," *The Boston Globe* (September 9, 2009), http://www.boston.com/business/articles/2009/09/09/sonic_barrier_broken/.
10. "Menu," *Sonic,* https://www.sonicdrivein.com/menu.

Chapter 9

1. Rance Crain, "Sir John Hegarty on How the Ad Industry Has Lost Its Courage, *Advertising Age* (September 15, 2014): 70.
2. *Merriam-Webster Unabridged Collegiate Dictionary*, s.v. "root," http://unabridged.merriam-webster.com/collegiate/root.
3. Mathew E. May, *The Elegant Solution: Toyota's Formula for Mastering Innovation* (New York: Free Press, 2007), 23.

Chapter 10

1. "Brazil: Atlantic Forest," *The Nature Conservancy*, accessed October 21, 2014, http://www.nature.org/ourinitiatives/regions/southamerica/brazil/placesweprotect/atlantic-forest.xml.

Chapter 11

1. Robert A. Lutz, *Guts: The Seven Laws of Business That Made Chrysler the World's Hottest Car Company* (Hoboken, NJ: John Wiley & Sons, 1998), 65–69.
2. Walter Isaacson, *Steve Jobs* (New York: Simon & Schuster, 2011), 371–73.
3. Brad Tuttle, "The 5 Big Mistakes That Led to Ron Johnson's Ouster at JC Penney," *Time* (April 9, 2013), http://business.time.com/2013/04/09/the-5-big-mistakes-that-led-to-ron-johnsons-ouster-at-jc-penney/.
4. Despair, Inc., accessed November 3, 2014, http://www.despair.com/.
5. From an exhibit entitled *Artist to Icon: Early Photographs of Elvis, Dylan, and the Beatles,* viewed by Jim Poage at the National Heritage Museum, Lexington, Massachusetts, on March 22, 2004. The exhibit's photographs of Elvis Presley were by Alfred Wertheimer. The text at the exhibit was on plaques beside exhibit photographs and in recordings of comments by Wertheimer. Also see Alfred Wertheimer, *Elvis at 21: New York to Memphis* (San Raphael, CA: Insight Editions), 154, 161–63.
6. Leslie Kaufman and Christine Haughney, "Gift of GQ Magazine Prompts Outcry from Lands' End Customers," *The New York Times* (August 13, 2014), http://www.nytimes.com/2014/08/14/business/media/risque-promotion-prompts-outcry-from-lands-end-customers.html.

Chapter 12

1. Fogg Method, accessed February 28, 2015, http://www.foggmethod.
   com/. See also *Stanford Persuasive Tech Lab,* accessed February 28, 2015,
   http://captology.stanford.edu/.

Chapter 13

1. "Father Guido Sarducci's Five Minute University," YouTube
   video, 3:55, posted January 23, 2007, https://www.youtube.com/
   watch?v=kO8x8eoU3L4.
2. Alan Eyerly, "Scientist Richard Feynman the Heart of 'The Challenger
   Disaster,'" *Los Angeles Times* (September 13, 2013), http://www.latimes.
   com/entertainment/tv/showtracker/la-et-st-tv-fall-preview-challenger-
   disaster-20130915-story.html#page=1.
3. Christine Nelson, *Drawing Babar: Early Drafts and Watercolors* (New
   York: The Morgan Library & Museum, 2008).
4. Jean de Brunhoff, *The Story of Babar* (New York: Random House, 1961),
   20, 21.
5. Hergé, *The Blue Lotus* (New York: Little, Brown and Company, 1984), 6.
6. Hergé, *The Seven Crystal Balls* (Boston: Little, Brown and Company,
   1975), 58.
7. Michael Farr, *Tintin: The Complete Companion* (San Francisco: Last
   Gasp, 2002).
8. *Interpret Indigo: A Design Guide for Hotel Indigo Hotels* (Hotel Indigo,
   2009), http://www.hoteldesigns.net/library/1252278000/ING_2661_
   InterpretIndigo_P2_v7_2.pdf.
9. "Hotel Indigo Drives Momentum Through Strategy and Growth,"
   Hospitality Net (June 6, 2006), http://www.hospitalitynet.org/
   news/4027675.html.
10. "Aloft Montreal Airport Opens, Making Global Lifestyle Debut,"
    BusinessWire (June 5, 2008), http://www.businesswire.com/portal/site/
    google/?ndmViewId=news_view&newsId=20080605005339&newsLa
    ng=en. Also, this description is based on observations by Jim, who has
    visited the lobby area of the Aloft Hotel in Lexington, Massachusetts.

11. "Malcolm Gladwell," TED, accessed May 18, 2015, https://www.ted.com/speakers/malcolm_gladwell.

12. Lizzie Widdicombe, "Lululemon Yoga Clothes," *The New Yorker* (February 2, 2015): 19–20.

Chapter 14

1. Bill Watterson, *Calvin and Hobbes,* GoComics (January 10, 2015), accessed on January 10, 2015, http://www.gocomics.com/calvinandhobbes/2015/01/10/.

2. Trish Witkowski, "Folded Inspiration," YouTube video, https://www.youtube.com/foldfactory.

Chapter 15

1. Sonia Sotomayor, *My Beloved World* (New York: Alfred A. Knopf, 2013), 209–11.

INDEX

ABOUT THE AUTHORS

Jim Poage, Ph.D., is Founder/President of JLP Performance Consulting. His practice focuses on improving organization productivity and creating an emotional connection with customers. An expert on the interactions of technology and users, he has authored articles for business and technical journals and has spoken at numerous conferences. He holds a Ph.D. from Harvard University School of Engineering and Applied Sciences and an M.S. and B.S. in Electrical Engineering from Stanford. Jim lives in Lexington, MA.

Jennifer Poage is a fashion designer working on her M.A. at the London College of Fashion. Formerly she was an apparel technical designer for Reebok and adidas. She has a B.A. in Art History from Drew University, an A.A.S. in Fashion Studies from Parsons School of Design, and a Business Essentials Certificate from the University of North Carolina's Kenan Flagler Business School. Jennifer lives in London, United Kingdom.